Letts

Revision Notes

GCSE SUCCESS

Mathematics Foundation

Author
Fiona C Mapp

Series editor
Alan Brewerton

Every effort has been made to trace copyright holders and to obtain their permission for the use of copyright material. The authors and publishers will gladly receive information enabling them to rectify any error or omission in subsequent editions.

First published 1997
Reprinted 1998
New edition 1998
This edition 1999
Reprinted 1999

Letts Educational, 9–15 Aldine Street, London W12 8AW
Tel. 0208 740 2270
Fax 0208 740 2280

Editorial, design and production by Hart McLeod, Cambridge

British Library Cataloguing-in-Publication Data

A CIP record for this book is available from the British Library

ISBN 1 84085 292 5

Printed and bound in UK by Ashford Colour Press

Letts Educational is the trading name of Letts Educational Ltd, a division of Granada Learning. Part of the Granada Media Group.

Acknowledgements
The author and publisher are grateful to the staff at Cottenham Village College, Cambridge, for their technical assistance.

Contents

Number and algebra

Shape, space and measures

Handling data

Introduction

This book has been specifically designed to help you prepare for your GCSE exams in the easiest and most effective way. Keep this book with you throughout your revision – it is the key to your success.

How to use this book

All the information you need to know for your course is presented as a series of brief facts and explanations. these will help you understand and remember your work. You can work through the book chapter by chapter or you can find individual topics by using the index at the back of the book. The example below shows how pages are organised to help you revise each topic.

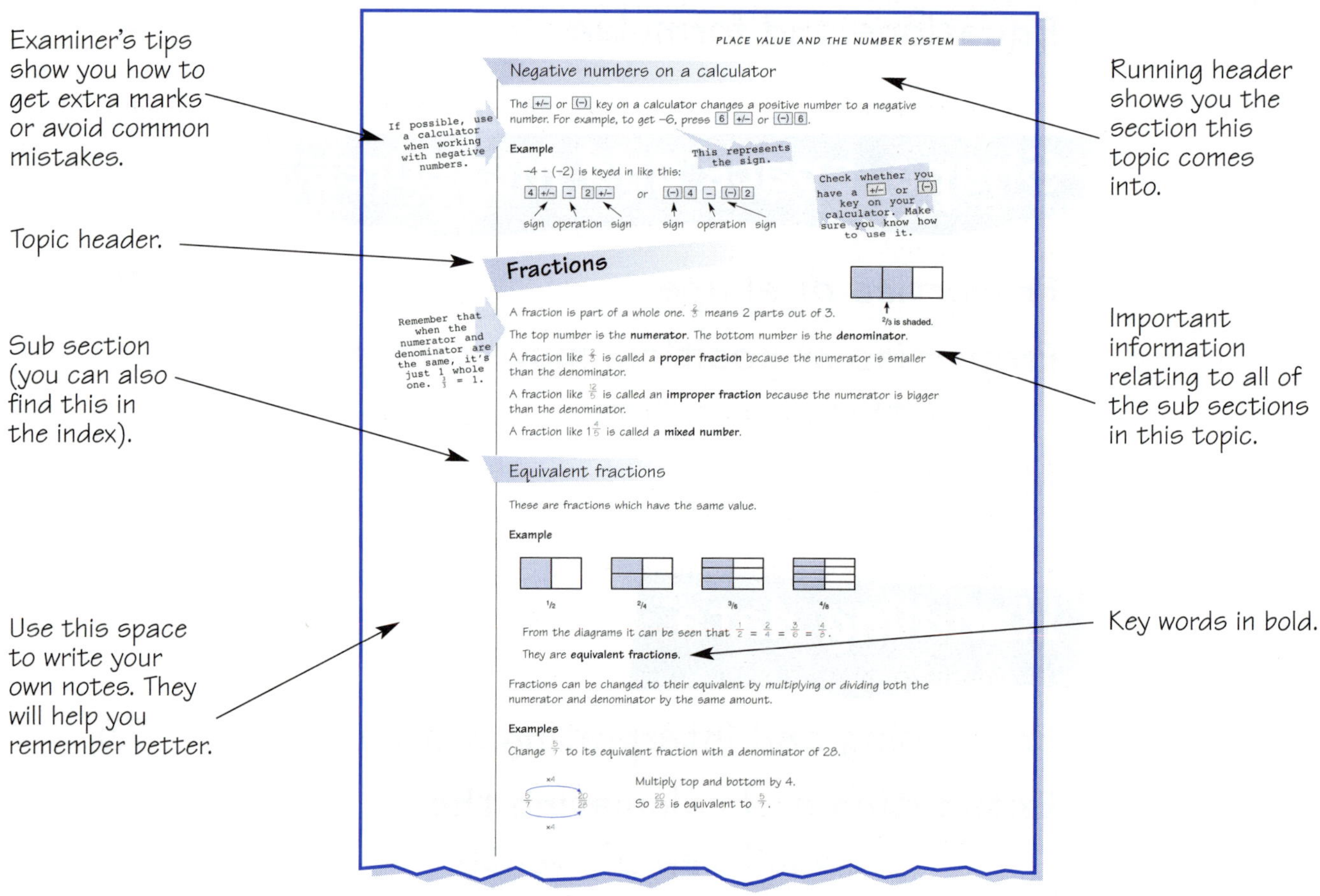

Preparing your revision programme

In most subjects you will have coursework, homework, revision, practice examination questions and a final examination. The examination may cause you the most anxiety. With proper preparation, however, you do not need to worry. Remember that there is a short test at the end of each topic. This test will help your understanding and boost your memory. Make sure that you have allowed enough time to revise your work and make a list of all the things you have to do and your coursework deadlines.

The examiner's report

Every year the examination boards publish reports on the previous year's examinations. The reports show areas in the examinations where students have performed well or badly and highlights mistakes that students frequently make. The examiners' reports can help you avoid making mistakes and therefore gain extra marks. **Recent examiners' reports highlight the following areas where students lost marks.**

- Lack of appropriate equipment, for example protractors, compasses and rulers.
- Insufficient, confused or no working out.
- Lack of units and poor accuracy.
- Vague answers with little reference to the data when answering questions which ask you to 'Explain'.
- Lack of knowledge of metric and imperial conversions.
- Poor skills in algebraic manipulation, e.g. the ability to form and solve equations.

Common areas of difficulty

Some common areas of difficulty on Foundation Level examination papers have occurred in the following topics:

- Long multiplication and division *page* 17
- Fractions *pages* 18–20
- Proportional changes with percentages *pages* 20–21
- Ratio calculations *pages* 21–22
- Estimates and approximations *page* 23
- Speed *pages* 30–31
- Graph drawing *pages* 36–37
- Distance–time graphs *pages* 39–40
- Multiplying out brackets *pages* 44–45
- Using equations to solve problems *pages* 47–48
- Angles in polygons *page* 56
- Transformations *pages* 59–62
- Reading scales *page* 67
- Area of complicated shapes *page* 69
- Pie charts *pages* 77–78
- Averages from a frequency table *pages* 83–84
- Relative frequency *page* 88

Most of all: **Good luck with your revision and your examinations.**

Number and algebra

Place value and the number system

Numbers

Examiner's tips and your notes

Each digit in a number has a **place value**.

The size of a number depends on its place value.

60

The place value is **ten** for this digit 6.

ten millions	millions	hundred thousands	ten thousands	thousands	hundreds	tens	units	
						5	7	fifty-seven
					4	9	5	four hundred and ninety-five
				3	2	8	6	three thousand, two hundred and eighty-six
			5	2	6	0	0	fifty-two thousand, six hundred
		1	2	4	3	2	0	one hundred and twenty-four thousand, three hundred and twenty
	4	6	2	9	0	3	6	four million, six hundred and twenty-nine thousand, and thirty-six

Make sure that you can write big numbers using words only.

These gaps make big numbers easier to read.

Always read the numbers from left to right.

Ordering numbers

- When putting numbers into order of size, first put the numbers into groups with the same number of digits.
- For each group, arrange the numbers in order of size depending on the place value of the digits.

Example

Arrange these numbers in order of size, smallest first.

26, 502, 794, 3627, 4209, 4390, 7, 86, 28, 114

Put into groups first.

7 (1 digit), 26, 86, 28 (2 digits), 502, 794, 114 (3 digits), 3627, 4209, 4390 (4 digits)

Check that you have included all numbers.

Arrange in order of size.

7, 26, 28, 86, 114, 502, 794, 3627, 4209, 4390

Rounding numbers to the nearest ten, hundred, thousand

Large numbers are often approximated to the nearest ten, hundred, thousand etc.

Rounding to the nearest ten

Look at the digit in the **units** column.

If it is less than 5, round down.

If it is 5 or more, round up.

Example Round 427 to the nearest ten.

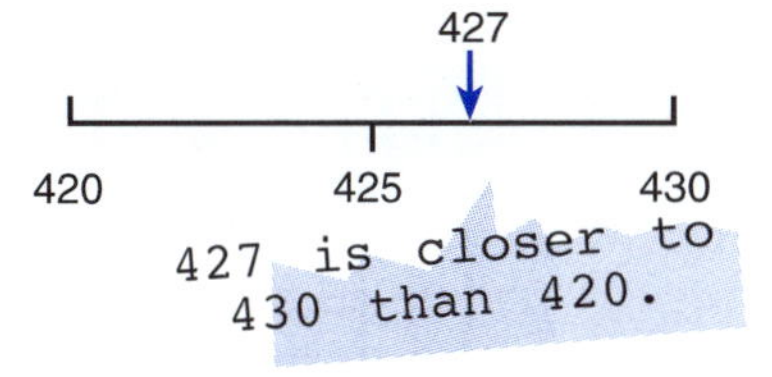

There is a 7 in the units column, so round up to 430.

Rounding to the nearest hundred

Look at the digit in the **tens** column.

If it is less than 5, round down.

If it is 5 or more, round up.

Example Round 1350 to the nearest hundred.

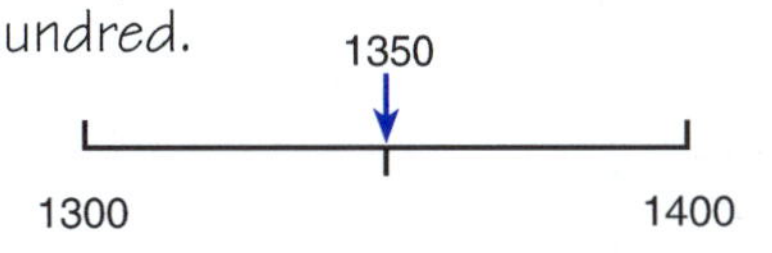

There is a 5 in the tens column, so round up to 1400.

1350 is 1400 to the nearest hundred.

Rounding to the nearest thousand

Look at the digit in the **hundreds** column. The same rules apply as before.

Sketch a number line if it helps.

Example Round 15 720 to the nearest thousand.

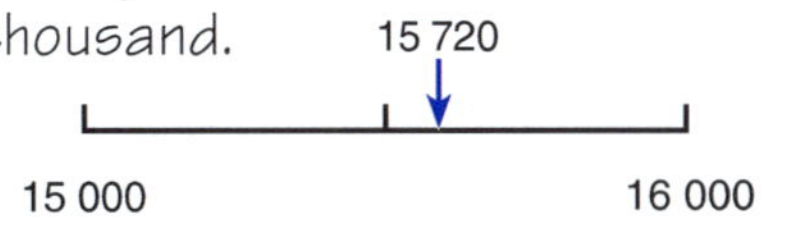

There is a 7 in the hundreds column, so round up to 16 000.

15 720 is 16 000 to the nearest thousand.

Directed numbers

These are numbers which may be positive or negative. **Positive** are above zero. **Negative** are below zero. Negative numbers have a minus (–) written in front of them.

Temperatures are a common example of directed numbers, e.g. –2 °C, 4 °C.

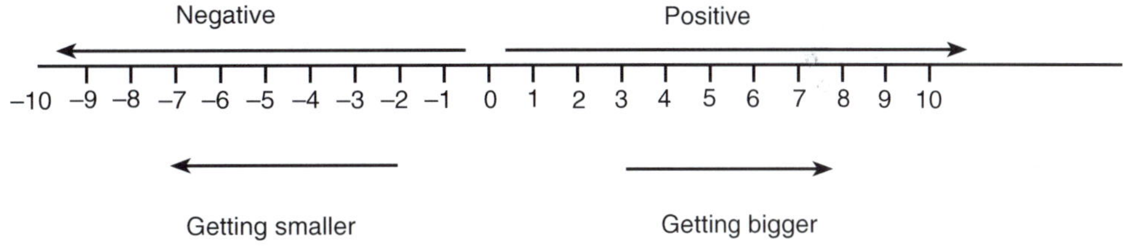

Examples

−10 is smaller than −8. −4 is bigger than −8. 2 is bigger than −6.

Example

Use the number line to help you arrange these numbers in order of size, smallest first: −9, −26, 12, 0, 4, −3, 2, 7

Arranged in order: −26, −9, −3, 0, 2, 4, 7, 12

Adding and subtracting directed numbers

When adding and subtracting directed numbers it is helpful to draw a number line.

Example

The temperature at 4 a.m. was −3 °C. By 11 a.m. it had risen by 7 degrees. What was the temperature at 11 a.m.?

Draw a number line to help you!

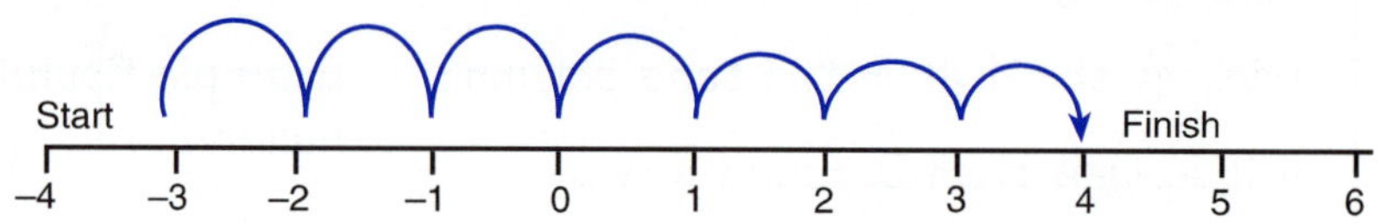

The temperature at 11 a.m. was 4 °C.

Example

Find the value of −3 − 5.

Note the different uses of the minus sign.

−3 − 5

This represents the **sign** of the number. (Start at −3.)

This represents the **operation** of subtraction. (Move 5 places to the left.)

−3 − 5 = −8

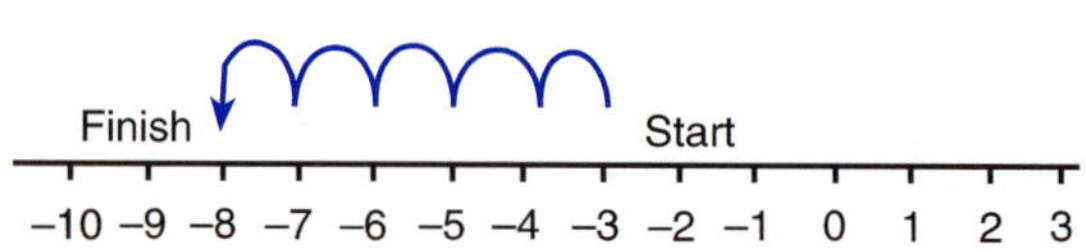

When the number to be added (or subtracted) is negative, the normal direction of movement is reversed.

Example

The negative changes the direction.

Move 3 places to the right.

−4 − (−3) is the same as −4 + 3 = −1

When two + or two − signs are together, then these rules are used:

+ (+) → +, − (−) → + } **Like signs give a positive.**

+ (−) → −, − (+) → − } **Unlike signs give a negative.**

Examples

−6 + (−2) = −6 − 2 = −8

−2 − (+6) = −2 − 6 = −8

4 − (−3) = 4 + 3 = 7

9 + (−3) = 9 − 3 = 6

Negative numbers on a calculator

If possible, use a calculator when working with negative numbers.

The [+/–] or [(–)] key on a calculator changes a positive number to a negative number. For example, to get –6, press [6] [+/–] or [(–)] [6].

This represents the sign.

Example

–4 – (–2) is keyed in like this:

[4] [+/–] [–] [2] [+/–] or [(–)] [4] [–] [(–)] [2]

sign operation sign sign operation sign

Check whether you have a [+/–] or [(–)] key on your calculator. Make sure you know how to use it.

Fractions

Remember that when the numerator and denominator are the same, it's just 1 whole one. $\frac{3}{3} = 1$.

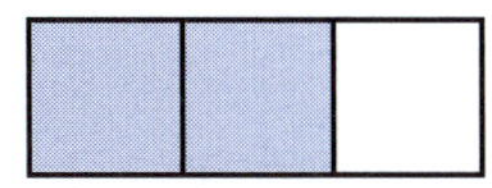

$^{2}/_{3}$ is shaded.

A fraction is part of a whole one. $\frac{2}{3}$ means 2 parts out of 3.

The top number is the **numerator**. The bottom number is the **denominator**.

A fraction like $\frac{2}{3}$ is called a **proper fraction** because the numerator is smaller than the denominator.

A fraction like $\frac{12}{5}$ is called an **improper fraction** because the numerator is bigger than the denominator.

A fraction like $1\frac{4}{5}$ is called a **mixed number**.

Equivalent fractions

These are fractions which have the same value.

Example

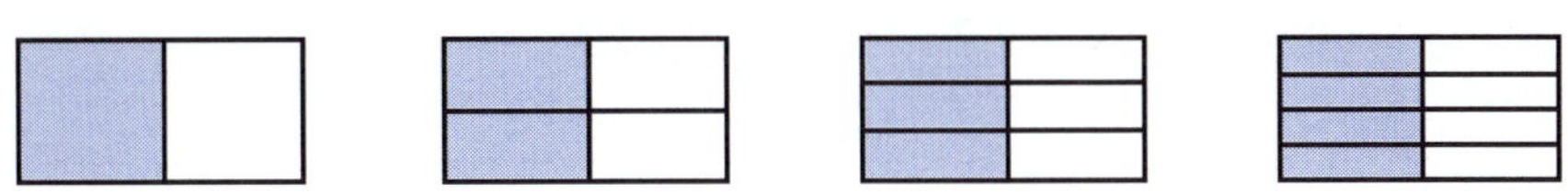

$^{1}/_{2}$ $^{2}/_{4}$ $^{3}/_{6}$ $^{4}/_{8}$

From the diagrams it can be seen that $\frac{1}{2} = \frac{2}{4} = \frac{3}{6} = \frac{4}{8}$.

They are **equivalent fractions**.

Fractions can be changed to their equivalent by *multiplying* or *dividing* both the numerator and denominator by the same amount.

Examples

Change $\frac{5}{7}$ to its equivalent fraction with a denominator of 28.

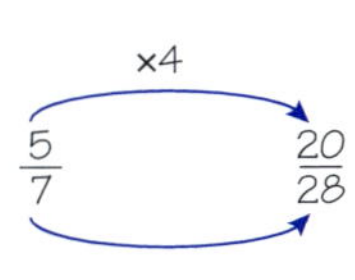

Multiply top and bottom by 4.

So $\frac{20}{28}$ is equivalent to $\frac{5}{7}$.

Equivalent fractions are useful when adding and subtracting with fractions.

Change $\frac{40}{60}$ to its equivalent fraction with a denominator of 3.

$$\frac{40}{60} \xrightarrow{\div 20} \frac{2}{3}$$

Divide top and bottom by 20.

So $\frac{40}{60}$ is equivalent to $\frac{2}{3}$.

Simplifying fractions

Fractions can be **simplified** if the numerator and denominator have a common factor.

A factor is a number which divides exactly into another number.

Example

Simplify $\frac{12}{18}$.

6 is the highest factor of both 12 and 18. Divide both the top and bottom numbers by 6.

$$\frac{12}{18} \xrightarrow{\div 6} \frac{2}{3}$$

So $\frac{12}{18}$ is simplified to $\frac{2}{3}$.

Using the fraction key on a calculator

If possible use the fraction key when simplifying. It's easier!

The [a b/c] key on *most* calculators is the fraction key.

$\frac{12}{18}$ is keyed in as 12 [a b/c] 18.

This is displayed as [12⌟18] or [12r18].

Pressing the [=] key on the calculator will automatically simplify fractions.

$\frac{12}{18}$ becomes [2⌟3] or [2r3].

These mean two-thirds.

A display of [1⌟4⌟9] or [1r4r9] means $1\frac{4}{9}$.

Pressing the [Shift] [a b/c] keys converts $1\frac{4}{9}$ back to an improper fraction, $\frac{13}{9}$ [13⌟9].

Decimals

A decimal point is used to separate whole-number columns from fractional columns.

Remember hundredths are smaller than tenths. $\frac{10}{100} = \frac{1}{10}$, so $\frac{6}{100} < \frac{1}{10}$.

Example

thousands	hundreds	tens	units		tenths	hundredths	thousandths
5	9	2	4	•	1	6	3

↑ decimal point

- The 1 means $\frac{1}{10}$.
- The 6 means $\frac{6}{100}$.
- The 3 means $\frac{3}{1000}$.

Recurring decimals

A decimal that **recurs** is shown by placing a dot over the numbers that repeat.

Examples

$0.3333... = 0.\dot{3}$ $0.1777... = 0.1\dot{7}$ $0.232323... = 0.\dot{2}\dot{3}$

Ordering decimals

When ordering decimals:

- Write them with the same number of figures after the decimal point.
- Then compare whole numbers, digits in the tenths place, digits in the hundredths place, and so on.

Example

Arrange the following in order of size, smallest first:

6.21, 6.023, 6.4, 6.04, 2.71, 9.4

Always check at the end that all values have been included.

First, rewrite as 6.210, 6.023, 6.400, 6.040, 2.710, 9.400

Then compare whole numbers, digits in the tenths place, and so on. This gives

2.710, 6.023, 6.040, 6.210, 6.400, 9.400

The 2 is smaller than the 4 so 6.023 is smaller than 6.040.

Decimal places (d.p.)

The number 12.437 256 has 6 decimal places because there are 6 numbers *after* the decimal point.

When rounding numbers to a specified number of decimal places:

- Look at the last number that is needed (if rounding 12.367 to 2 d.p. look at the 6 which is in the second decimal place).
- Look at the number on its right (look at the number which is not needed, the 7).
- If the number which is not needed is **5 or more**, then **round up** the last digit. (7 is greater than a 5 so round up the 6 to a 7.)
- If the digit is less than 5, then **the digit remains the same**.

Examples

Round 12.49 to 1 d.p.

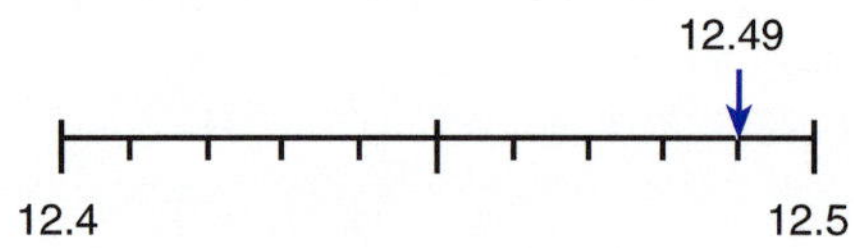

12.4**9** rounds up to 12.5.

Round 8.735 to 2 d.p.

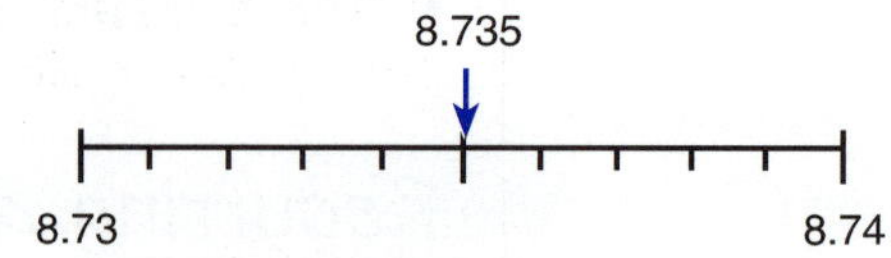

8.7**35** rounds up to 8.74.

Percentages

These are fractions with a **denominator of 100**.

% is the percentage sign. 60% means $\frac{60}{100}$.

Ratios

A ratio is used to compare two or more related quantities.

'**Compared to**' is replaced with **two dots:** For example, '16 boys compared to 20 girls' can be written as 16 : 20.

If possible use your calculator fraction key to simplify ratios, in the same way as fractions.

To simplify ratios, divide both parts of the ratio by the highest factor.
For example, 16 : 20 = 4 : 5 (Divide both sides by 4.)

Example

Simplify the ratio 21 : 28. 21 : 28 = 3 : 4 (Divide both sides by 7.)

Equivalences between fractions, decimals and percentages

Fractions, decimals and percentages all mean the same thing but are just written in a different way:

Fraction		Decimal		Percentage
$\frac{1}{2}$	$\xrightarrow{1 \div 2}$	0.5	$\xrightarrow{\times 100\%}$	50%
$\frac{3}{5}$		0.6		60%
$\frac{7}{10}$		0.7		70%
$\frac{1}{3}$		$0.\dot{3}$		$33.\dot{3}\%$

Ordering different numbers

When putting fractions, decimals and percentages in order of size, it is best to change them all to **decimals** first.

Example

Place in order of size, smallest first:

Make sure you put the values in the order the question says.

$\frac{3}{5}$, 0.65, 0.273, 27%, 62%, $\frac{4}{9}$

$0.6, 0.65, 0.273, 0.27, 0.62, 0.4\dot{4}$ Put into decimals first.

$0.27, 0.273, 0.4\dot{4}, 0.6, 0.62, 0.65$ Now order.

27%, 0.273, $\frac{4}{9}$, $\frac{3}{5}$, 62%, 0.65 Now rewrite them back in their orignal form.

Index notation

An **index** is sometimes known as a **power**.

3^5 is read as **3 to the power 5**. It means 3 × 3 × 3 × 3 × 3.

2^6 is read as **2 to the power 6**. It means 2 × 2 × 2 × 2 × 2 × 2.

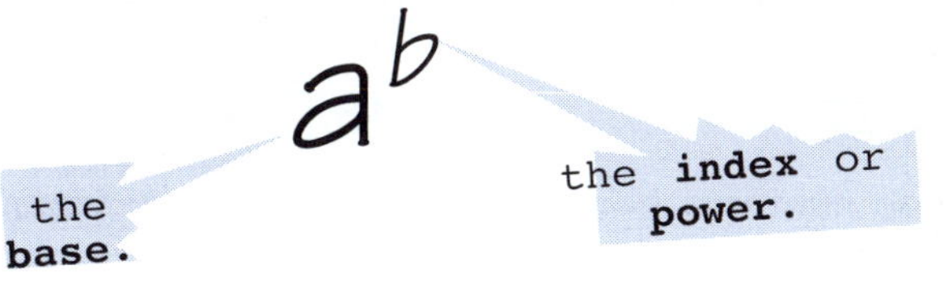

The **base** is the value which has to be multiplied. The **index** indicates how many times.

Powers on a calculator display

The value 4×10^9 means

4 × 10 × 10 × 10 × 10 × 10 × 10 × 10 × 10 × 10 = 4 000 000 000.

On a calculator display 4×10^9 looks like [4 09]

and 5×10^{13} looks like [5 13].

Questions

1 Write the number 2 462 004 in words.

2 Round these numbers to the nearest 10:

(a) 62 (b) 87 (c) 145

3 Round these numbers to the nearest 100:

(a) 1279 (b) 604

4 Round these numbers to the nearest 1000:

(a) 6449 (b) 7860

5 The temperature at 4 a.m. was −9 °C and it rose by 15 degrees. What was the new temperature?

6 Work out the following:

(a) $-2 + 4$ (b) $-6 - 3$ (c) $3 + (-9)$

7 Write these out in full:

(a) 4^6 (b) 3^4

8 Write down what this calculator display means. 6^{15}

9 Change these fractions to their equivalents:

(a) $\frac{2}{9} = \frac{?}{27}$ (b) $\frac{12}{16} = \frac{3}{?}$

10 Write these numbers in order of size, smallest first:

6.43, 0.63, 4.89, 4.07, 8.31, 10.7, 8.295

11 Write 17% as a fraction.

12 A class has 39% boys in it. What percentage are girls?

13 Simplify the following ratios:

(a) 12 : 18 (b) 27 : 9 (c) 30 : 15

14 Convert $\frac{4}{5}$ into: (a) a decimal (b) a percentage

15 Round 14.638 to two decimal places.

16 Round 9.35 to one decimal place.

Relationships between numbers and computation methods

Types of number

Examiner's tips and your notes

Odd numbers are numbers which 2 does not divide into exactly. All odd numbers end in 1, 3, 5, 7 or 9.

Even numbers are numbers which all divide exactly by 2. All even numbers end in 0, 2, 4, 6 or 8.

Multiples are just the numbers in multiplication tables. For example,

multiples of 6 are 6, 12, 18, 24, 30, . . .

Factors are whole numbers which divide exactly into another number.

Example

The factors of 20 are 1, 2, 4, 5, 10, 20.

Factors of 20 can be arranged into **factor pairs**.

Start at 20 and divide all the numbers in turn to obtain all the factors of 20.

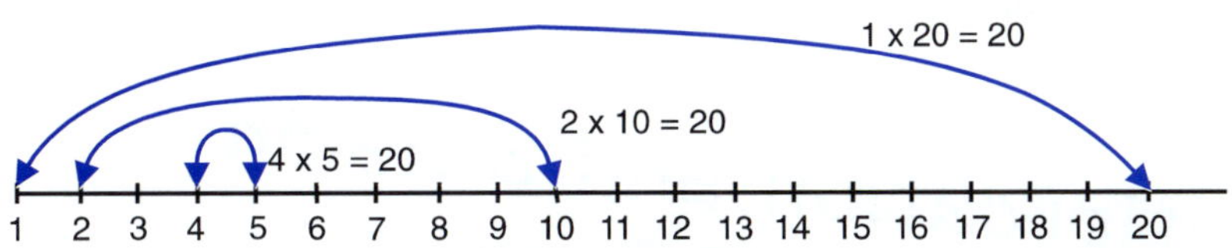

Prime numbers are numbers which only have two factors, **1 and itself**.

Make sure you know the prime numbers up to 20.

Remember 1 is **not** a prime number. The smallest prime number is 2, which is also the only even prime number.

Prime numbers up to 20 are 2, 3, 5, 7, 11, 13, 17, 19.

Squares and cubes

Square numbers

Anything to the **power 2** is **square**. For example, $6^2 = 6 \times 6 = 36$ (six squared).

Square numbers include:

1	4	9	16	25	36	49	64	81	100	. . .
(1 x 1)	(2 x 2)	(3 x 3)	(4 x 4)	(5 x 5)	(6 x 6)	(7 x 7)	(8 x 8)	(9 x 9)	(10 x 10)	

Square numbers can be illustrated by drawing squares.

It is important that you can recognise square and cube numbers.

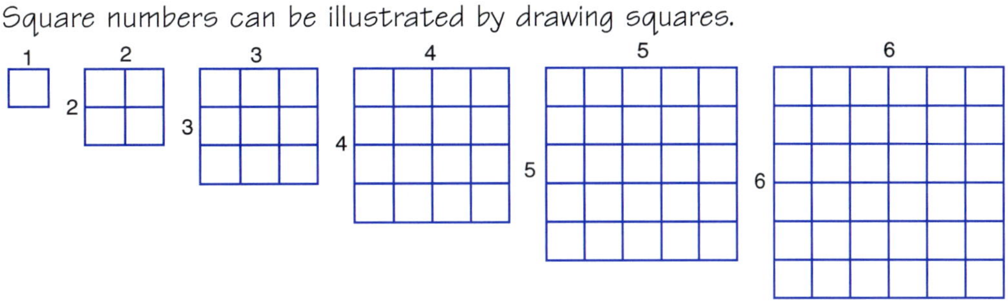

Cube numbers

Anything to the **power 3** is **cube**. For example, $5^3 = 5 \times 5 \times 5 = 125$ (five cubed).

Cube numbers include:

1	8	27	64	125	216	...
(1 × 1 × 1)	(2 × 2 × 2)	(3 × 3 × 3)	(4 × 4 × 4)	(5 × 5 × 5)	(6 × 6 × 6)	

Cube numbers can be illustrated by drawing cubes.

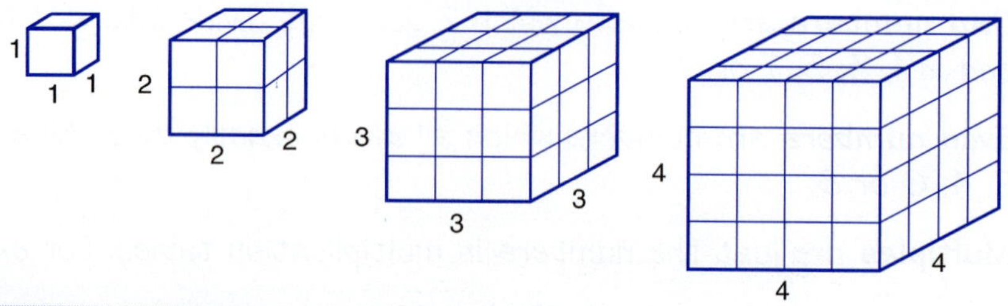

Square roots and cube roots

If possible, use a calculator to find a square root of a number.

$\sqrt{}$ is the **square root sign**. Taking the square root is the opposite of squaring.

For example, $\sqrt{25} = 5$ since $5^2 = 25$.

$\sqrt[3]{}$ is the **cube root sign**. Taking the cube root is the opposite of cubing.

For example, $\sqrt[3]{8} = 2$ since $2^3 = 8$.

Multiplication and division by 10, 100, 1000 etc.

To **multiply** by 10, 100, 1000 etc., move the decimal point one, two, three etc. places to the right, or put in zeros if necessary.

Examples

16.2 × 10 = 162 42 × 10 = 420	Move the decimal point one place to the right. Put in a zero.
16.2 × 100 = 1620 42 × 100 = 4200	Move the decimal point two places to the right. Put in two zeros.
16.2 × 1000 = 16200 42 × 1000 = 42000	Move the decimal point three spaces to the right. Put in three zeros.

To **divide** by 10, 100, 1000 etc. move the decimal point one, two, three etc. places to the left.

Examples

16.2 ÷ 10 = 1.62   42 ÷ 100 = 0.42   17.4 ÷ 1000 = 0.0174

When multiplying by multiples of 10 (20, 30, 700 etc.) the same rules apply, except you multiply the numbers first then move the decimal point to the right.

Examples

60 × 40 = 2400 — 6 × 4 = 24, then move the decimal point two places to the right.

42 × 20 = 840

When dividing by multiples of 10 the same rules apply, except you divide the numbers and then move the decimal point to the left.

Examples

4000 ÷ 20 = 200 — 4 ÷ 2 = 2, then move the decimal point 1 place to the left.

630 ÷ 30 = 21

Long multiplication

For long multiplication and division questions, check your answer with a calculator.

```
   274
    26 ×
 1 6₄4₂4      Step 1   274 × 6
 5₁4 8 0 +    Step 2   274 × 20
 7 1 2 4      Step 3   1644 + 5480
  1 1
```

Long division

```
       23
 15 ) 345
      30 −
       45
       45 −
        0
```

Step 1	15 goes into 34 twice. Write down the 2.
Step 2	15 × 2 = 30. Place below the 34.
Step 3	Subtract 30 from 34.
Step 4	Bring down the 5.
Step 5	Divide 45 by 15. Write down the 3.
Step 6	15 × 3 = 45. Place below the 45.
Step 7	45 − 45 = 0

So 345 ÷ 15 = 23

```
       16
 12 ) 195
      12 −
       75
       72 −
        3
```

So 195 ÷ 12 = 16 remainder 3

Sufficient working needs to be shown in order to obtain full marks at GCSE.

Calculations with decimals

When adding and subtracting decimals, the decimal points need to go under each other.

Line up the digits carefully.

Examples

```
 27.46
  7.291 +
 34.751
 1  1
```

Put the decimal points under each other.

The decimal point in the answer will be in line.

```
  6 9 1
 1̸7̸.0̸0
 12.84 −
  4.16
```

Remember to put the decimal points under each other.

Remember to check with your calculator.

When **multiplying** decimals, the answer must have the same number of decimal places as the total number of decimal places in the numbers which are being multiplied.

Examples

```
 24.6
    7 ×
172.2
```

Multiply 246 by 7 = 1722, ignoring the decimal point.
24.6 has 1 number after the decimal point.
The answer must have 1 decimal place (1 d.p.).

So 24.6 × 7 = 172.2

Work out 4.52 × 0.2

```
452
  2 ×
904
```

Work out 452 × 2, ignoring the decimal points.
4.52 has 2 d.p. 0.2 has 1 d.p. So the answer must have 3 d.p.

904 → 0.904 Move the decimal point 3 places.

So 4.52 × 0.2 = 0.904

When **dividing** decimals, divide as normal, placing the decimal points in line.

Example

```
   4.8
3 |14.4
```

Put the decimal points in line.

Fractions

When the numerator is **less than** the denominator, it is a **proper fraction**.

When the numerator is **bigger than** the denominator, it is an **improper fraction**.

$2\frac{1}{2}$ is called a **mixed number**.

Addition and subtraction of fractions

The examples show the basic principles of adding and subtracting fractions.

Example

$\frac{1}{8} + \frac{3}{4}$

- First make the denominators the same.
  $\frac{3}{4}$ is **equivalent** to $\frac{6}{8}$.

$\frac{3}{4} = \frac{6}{8}$ (× 2 numerator, × 2 denominator)

$= \frac{1}{8} + \frac{6}{8}$

- Replace $\frac{3}{4}$ with $\frac{6}{8}$ so that the denominators are now the same.

$= \frac{7}{8}$

- Add the numerators $1 + 6 = 7$.
- **Do not add** the denominators.
- The denominator stays the same number.

If you have a fraction key on your calculator, use it as a check.

Example

$\frac{3}{4} - \frac{3}{16}$

- First make the denominators the same.
  $\frac{3}{4}$ is **equivalent** to $\frac{12}{16}$.

$\frac{3}{4} \xrightarrow{\times 4} \frac{12}{16}$ (numerator × 4, denominator × 4)

$= \frac{12}{16} - \frac{3}{16}$

- Replace $\frac{3}{4}$ with $\frac{12}{16}$.

$= \frac{9}{16}$

- Subtract the numerators but **not** the denominators.
- The denominator stays the same number.

If possible use the fraction key on the calculator, like this.

3 [a b/c] 4 [−] 3 [a b/c] 16 [=]

Multiplication and division of fractions

When multiplying and dividing fractions, write out whole or mixed numbers as improper fractions before starting. For example, rewrite $2\frac{1}{2}$ as $\frac{5}{2}$.

Example

$\frac{4}{7} \times \frac{2}{11} = \frac{8}{77}$

← Multiply the numerators together.

← Multiply the denominators together.

For division change it into a multiplication by turning the second fraction upside down and multiplying both fractions together.

If you have a calculator with a fraction key use it to check!

Example

$\frac{7}{9} \div \frac{12}{18}$

Turn the $\frac{12}{18}$ upside down and multiply with the $\frac{7}{9}$.

$= \frac{7}{9} \times \frac{18}{12} = \frac{126}{108} = 1\frac{1}{6}$

Rewrite back as a mixed number.

Example

$2\frac{1}{2} \div \frac{7}{9}$

Change $2\frac{1}{2}$ into an improper fraction, $\frac{5}{2}$.

$= \frac{5}{2} \div \frac{7}{9}$

$= \frac{5}{2} \times \frac{9}{7} = \frac{45}{14} = 3\frac{3}{14}$

Turn the second fraction upside down and multiply with the $\frac{5}{2}$.

Fractions of a quantity

The word **of** means **multiply**.

Remember to put the units on your answer.

You could use your fraction key if you have one.

Example

Find $\frac{2}{3}$ of £27.

Rewrite as $\frac{2}{3} \times £27 = £18$.

On the calculator key in 2 ÷ 3 × 27 =

Percentages

Percentages of a quantity

Remember that a % is a fraction with a denominator of 100.

Replace 'of' with the × sign. Rewrite the percentage as a fraction.

Example

What is 40% of £800?

$\frac{40}{100} \times £800 = £320$

On the calculator key in 40 ÷ 100 × 800 =

One quantity as a percentage of another

To make the answer a percentage, multiply by **100%**.

Questions involving percentages appear on the exam paper every year and so it is important to be aware of the various techniques required.

Make a fraction with the two numbers.

Multiply by 100% to get a percentage.

Example

In a maths test Matthew got 64 out of 82. What percentage did he get?

$\frac{64}{82} \times 100\% = 78\%$

On the calculator key in 64 ÷ 82 × 100 =

Proportional changes with fractions and percentages

Fractions and percentages often appear in real-life problems.

Example

Last year there were 1 290 pupils on roll at Skatty High School. This year the school roll was increased by $\frac{2}{5}$. How many pupils are now on the school roll?

$\frac{2}{5} \times 1\,290 = 516$ — Work out $\frac{2}{5}$ of 1 290 pupils (this is the increase).

$1\,290 + 516 = 1\,806$ pupils — Add on the increase to the original number.

Always check that you answer the question.

Example

A travel company offers 15% off all holiday prices. How much would it cost for a two-week holiday in Spain which originally cost £642?

$\frac{15}{100} \times £642 = £96.30$ — Work out 15% of £642 to find the reduction.

Always check your answer sounds sensible.

New price = £642 − £96.30 = £545.70 — Subtract the reduction from the original price.

Example

A shop buys some jumpers at £18. The shop sells the jumpers for 30% more. What is the selling price of the jumpers?

$\frac{30}{100} \times 18 = £5.40$ — Work out the 30% increase.

Selling price = £18 + £5.40 = £23.40 — Add the increase on to its original price.

Ratio calculations

Sharing a quantity in a given ratio

- Add up the total parts.
- Work out what one part is worth.
- Work out what the other parts are worth.

Example

Emily and Imran share £140 in the ratio 3 : 4. How much does each person get?

Check by adding the amount of money each receives. This should equal the amount of money shared out.

3 + 4 = 7 parts

7 parts = £140 1 part = $\frac{£140}{7}$ = £20

So Emily gets 3 × £20 = £60 (3 lots of £20)

Imran gets 4 × £20 = £80

Increasing and decreasing in a given ratio

- Divide to get one part.
- Multiply for each new part.

Example

12 oranges cost 72p. How much do 5 similar oranges cost?

Cost of 12 oranges = 72p

Cost of 1 orange = $\frac{72p}{12}$ = 6p — Find the cost of 1 orange.

Cost of 5 oranges = 5 × 6p = 30p — Multiply the cost of 1 orange by 5 to find the cost of 5 oranges.

Example

A house took 8 people 6 days to build. At the same rate how long would it take 3 people?

Time for 8 people = 6 days

Time for 1 person = 8 × 6 = 48 days — It takes 1 person longer to build the house.

Time for 3 people = $\frac{48}{3}$ = 16 days — 3 people will take $\frac{1}{3}$ of the time taken by 1 person.

Example

Recipe questions are very common at GCSE.

A recipe for 4 people needs 1 600g of flour. How much is needed for 6 people?

Divide 1 600g by 4, so 400g for 1 person.

Multiply by 6, so 6 × 400g = 2 400g for 6 people.

Example

A photograph of length 9 cm is to be enlarged in the ratio 5 : 3. What is the length of the enlarged photograph?

Divide 9 cm by 3 to get 1 part, so 9 ÷ 3 = 3 cm.

Multiply by 5, so 5 × 3 = 15 cm on the enlarged photograph.

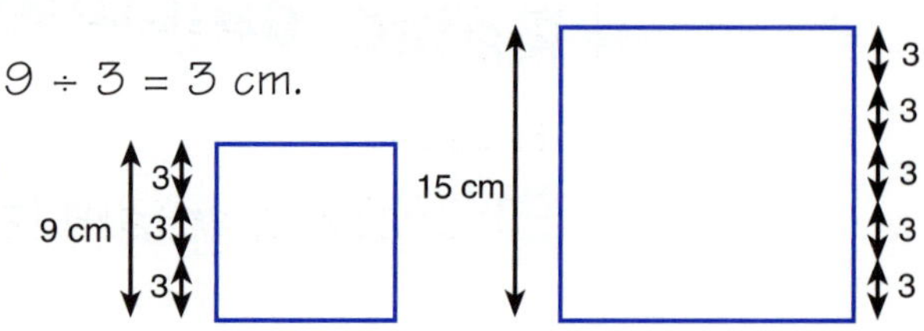

Using a calculator

Order of operations

BODMAS is a made-up word which helps you to remember the order in which calculations take place.

B	O	D	M	A	S
Brackets	Over	Division	Multiplication	Addition	Subtraction

This just means that brackets are worked out first, then the others are done in order.

Example

2 + 6 × 3 = 20 (not 24) because 6 × 3 = 18 and 18 + 2 = 20.

Multiplication is done **before** addition.

Example

(3 + 6) × 4 = 9 × 4 = 36 — Brackets are done first.

Important calculator keys

Make sure that you know how your calculator works!

(−) or +/− change positive numbers to negative ones.

C this only cancels the last key which was pressed.

AC this cancels all of the work.

√ square root key.

x^2 square key on some calculators.

Shift 2nd Inv These allow second functions to be carried out. Each calculator key is the main function. The second function is usually above it.

a^b/c fraction key on some calculators.

If possible use the C key as it saves lots of time.

When using a calculator:

- Press the keys slowly and carefully.
- If the incorrect key is pressed, clear it by using C instead of AC.
- Always press the = key after each calculation.

Example

Using a calculator, work out $\frac{\sqrt{32} + 3.2}{4.6}$, giving your answer to 1 decimal place.

$$\frac{\sqrt{32} + 3.2}{4.6} = 1.9 \text{ (1 d.p.)}$$

Check that you obtain this answer. Write down the calculator keys you use.

Estimates and approximations

Estimating is a good way of checking answers.

- Round the numbers to easier numbers, usually to the nearest 10, 100 etc.
- Work out the estimated answer using these easy numbers.
- Use the symbol ≈, which means '**is approximately equal to**'.

Example

Estimate the answer to 22 × 98.

$$22 \times 98 \approx 20 \times 100 = 2000$$

Round the 22 to 20 and the 98 to 100 to make the question easier to work out.

You must show your working out with your estimates to obtain full marks.

Example

Estimate the answer to $\frac{62 + 121}{29}$.

$$\frac{62 + 121}{29} \approx \frac{60 + 120}{30} = \frac{180}{30} = 6$$

Relationships between numbers and computation methods

Questions

1

1	2	3	4	5	6
7	8	9	10	11	12
13	14	15	16	17	18
19	20	21	22	23	24

From the numbers 1 to 24 write down:

(a) all the odd numbers

(b) all the even numbers

(c) all the prime numbers

(d) all the square numbers

(e) all the multiples of 7

(f) all the factors of 20

2 Work these out. (a) $\sqrt{64}$ (b) $\sqrt{81}$

3 Without a calculator work out these:

(a) 12.4×10 (b) 6.23×100 (c) 42×1000

(d) $24.6 \div 10$ (e) $273 \div 1000$ (f) 600×2000

4 Without a calculator work out these:

(a) $\begin{array}{r} 603 \\ \underline{45\ \times} \end{array}$ (b) $26\overline{)1066}$

5 Without a calculator work out these:

(a) $\begin{array}{r} 27.6 \\ \underline{2.79\ +} \end{array}$ (b) $\begin{array}{r} 12.3 \\ \underline{6.02\ -} \end{array}$ (c) $\begin{array}{r} 42.1 \\ \underline{3\ \times} \end{array}$ (d) $3\overline{)62.4}$

6 Find these: (a) $\frac{2}{9}$ of £36 (b) 26% of £42

7 Out of 42 people, 18 are girls. What percentage are girls?

8 A new car cost £9 725. Three years later it was sold at a 44% loss. How much was the car sold for?

9 Divide £420 in the ratio 2 : 6.

10 4 kg of potatoes cost £1.26. How much does 9 kg cost?

11 Without a calculator work out these.

(a) $9 \times 2 + 4$ (b) $(6 + 2) \times 3$

12 Estimate the answer to $\dfrac{61 \times 49}{29}$.

Solving numerical problems

Calculations

Examiner's tips and your notes

When solving problems you should round the answers sensibly.

Example

95.26 × 6.39 = 608.7114 = 608.71 (to 2 d.p.)

This is rounded to 2 decimal places because the values in the question are to 2 decimal places.

Example

Jim has £9.37. He divides it equally between 5 people. How much does each person receive?

£9.37 ÷ 5 = £1.874
= £1.87

Round to £1.87 since it is money.

Interpreting the calculator display with money problems

When questions involve money, remember the following:

- a display of 4.7 means £4.70 (four pounds seventy pence);
- a display of 4.07 means £4.07 (four pounds and seven pence);
- a display of 0.61 means £0.61 or 61 pence;
- a display of 4.75271 must be rounded to 2 d.p. to give £4.75.

You will lose marks if you do not put the zero at the end.

Checking calculations

Calculations can be checked by **estimating the answer**. This allows a rough idea of the size of the answer to be given.

Example

On her calculator Rhysian worked out the answer to 26 × 51. She thought it was 132. Is this correct?

Estimating gives 30 × 50 ≈ 1500. Rhysian's answer is not correct, it is 10 times too small. It is not the right **order of magnitude**.

Calculations can be checked by **applying the inverse process**.

Right order of magnitude means 'about the right size'.

Example

106 × 3 = 318

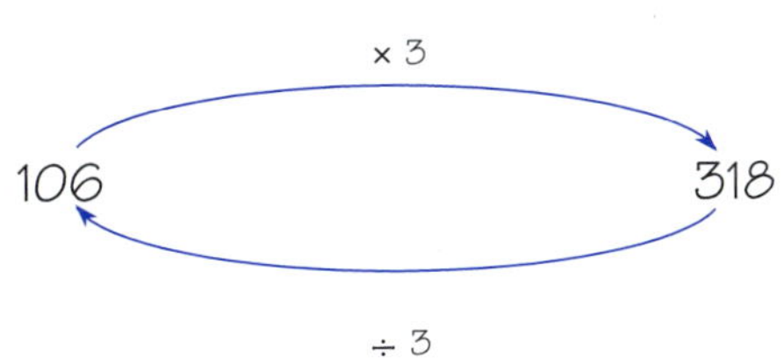

So 318 ÷ 3 = 106

Check calculations by quickly applying the inverse.

Trial and improvement

This is when successive approximations are made in order to get closer to the correct value.

Example

If $x^2 = 5$, use trial and improvement to find the value of x accurate to 1 decimal place.

Try $x = 2$	$2^2 = 2 \times 2 = 4$	(too small)
Try $x = 3$	$3^2 = 3 \times 3 = 9$	(too big)
Try $x = 2.5$	$2.5^2 = 2.5 \times 2.5 = 6.25$	(too big)
Try $x = 2.3$	$2.3^2 = 2.3 \times 2.3 = 5.29$	(too big)
Try $x = 2.2$	$2.2^2 = 2.2 \times 2.2 = 4.84$	(too small)

Remember x^2 means $x \times x$.

4.84 is closer to 5 than 5.29, so

$x = 2.2$ gives x^2 closer to 5 than $x = 2.3$.

Make sure you write down the value of x at the end.

Solving problems

The examination contains lots of problem-like questions where applications of percentages, fractions, decimals and ratios are needed.

Wages and salaries

Salaries are paid at a fixed amount per year.

Weekly wages are paid at a fixed amount per hour.

Overtime is usually paid at a different hourly rate, such as time and a half, double time etc.

Example

Colin usually works a 36-hour week at £6.20 per hour. One week he does 5 hours' overtime at time and a half and 3 hours' overtime at double time. How much does he earn at the end of that week?

Break down a question like this into stages. It makes it much easier.

Weekly wage = $36 \times £6.20 = £223.20$

Overtime pay at time and a half = $5 \times 1\frac{1}{2} \times £6.20 = £46.50$

5 hours at $1\frac{1}{2}$ times the normal rate

Overtime pay at double time = $3 \times 2 \times £6.20 = £37.20$

3 hours at $2 \times$ rate

Total wage = £223.20 + £46.50 + £37.20
= £306.90

Value added tax (VAT)

VAT is a tax which is added on to the cost of most items.

Example

A meal for four costs £92.20. VAT is charged at 17.5%.

(a) How much VAT is there to pay on the meal?

(b) What is the final price of the meal?

Remember to round money answers to 2 d.p.

(a) 17.5% of £92.20

$= \frac{17.5}{100} \times £92.20 = £16.14$ (to the nearest penny)

VAT = £16.14

(b) Price of meal = £92.20 + £16.14 = £108.34

This is just like a percentage of a quantity question.

Hire purchase (HP)

This is a common way of buying expensive items. When items are bought on HP, usually a deposit is paid followed by monthly instalments.

Example

A three-piece suite can either be bought for £899 cash or on hire purchase. If the suite is bought on hire purchase a 15% deposit followed by 12 monthly instalments of £68 is paid.

(a) How much does the three-piece suite cost on hire purchase?

(b) What is the difference between the prices for cash and for hire purchase?

(a) Cost of 15% deposit $= \frac{15}{100} \times £899 = £134.85$

Cost of monthly payments = 12 × £68
= £816

Total HP price = £134.85 + £816
= £950.85

(b) Difference = £950.85 – £899 = £51.85

For the 15% deposit, find 15% of the price.

Simple interest

This interest is sometimes paid on money in bank and building society savings accounts. The interest is paid each year (**per annum** or **p.a.**).

Example

Check you have answered the question.

Jerry has £4 000 in his bank account. Simple interest is paid at 5.2% p.a. How much does he have at the end of the year?

Interest = 5.2% of £4 000

$= \frac{5.2}{100} \times £4\,000 = £208$

So total in account = £4 000 + £208 = £4 208

If the money was in the bank for 5 years, then the interest at the end of 5 years would be 5 × £208 = £1040.

Tax

A percentage of the taxable part of a wage or salary is taken as **income tax**. Personal allowances must first be subtracted in order to obtain the **taxable income**.

Example

Susan earns £16 000 a year. Her first £3 255 is not taxable but the remainder is taxed at 25%. How much income tax does she pay?

This question is just the same as finding a percentage of a quantity.

Taxable income = £16 000 − £3 255
= £12 745

First remove the income which is not taxed.

Tax

25% of £12 745
$= \frac{25}{100} \times 12\,745 = £3\,186.25$

Tax is 25% of £12 745.

Foreign currency

The value of a single unit currency is called the **exchange rate**.

Example

Find the value of £700 in Canadian dollars if there are 2.04 Canadian dollars to the pound.

£1 = 2.04 Canadian dollars

£700 = 700 × 2.04 = 1 428 Canadian dollars

We have 700 lots of 2.04 Canadian dollars!

Example

On coming back from Canada I had 392 Canadian dollars left. Change this back into sterling.

The inverse operation can be applied here.

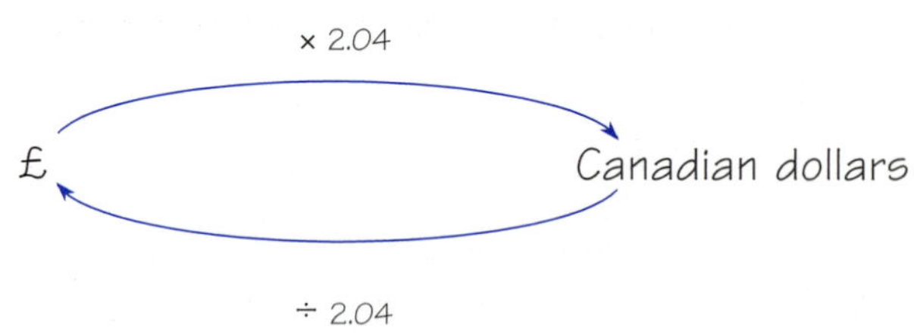

So 392 ÷ 2.04 = £192.16
(to the nearest penny)

Best buys

Unit amounts are looked at to decide which is the better value for money.

Example

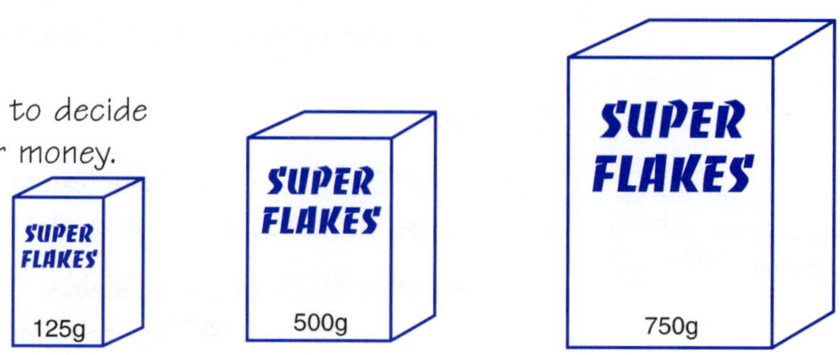

95p £1.58 £1.89

The same brand of breakfast cereal is sold in three different sized packets. Which packet represents the better value for money?

For these types of questions it is very important that each step in your working is shown so that you can clearly justify your answer.

Find the cost per gram for each packet:

125 g costs 95p. So unit cost = 95 ÷ 125 = 0.76p per gram.

500 g costs 158p. So unit cost = 158 ÷ 500 = 0.316p per gram.

750 g costs 189p. So unit cost = 189 ÷ 750 = 0.252p per gram.

Since the 750 g packet costs less per gram, it is the better value for money.

Time

12- and 24-hour clock times

The **12-hour clock** uses **a.m.** and **p.m.**

a.m. means **before midday**, p.m. means **after midday**.

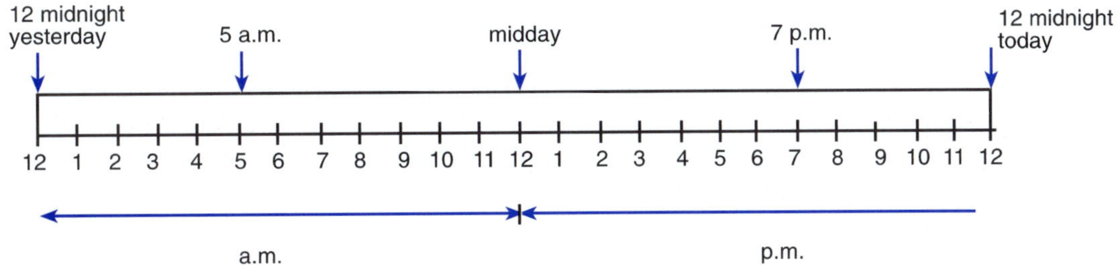

The **24-hour clock** numbers the hours from 0 to 23.
It is written using four figures.

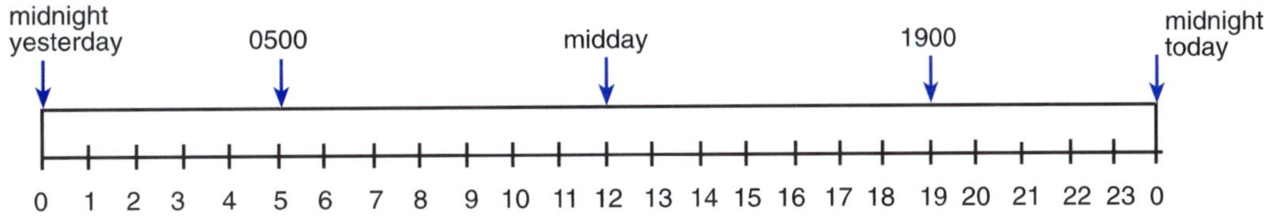

You need to be able to write times using both the 12-hour and 24-hour clock.

Examples

3:43 p.m. is the same as 1543.

2:30 a.m. is the same as 0230.

1334 is the same as 1:34 p.m.

1004 is the same as 10:04 a.m.

Remember to write in 'a.m.' and 'p.m.' for 12-hour clock times.

Calculations with times

When calculating with time, you need to work out the answers step by step.

Example

How long is a train journey if the train sets off at 1426 and arrives at its destination at 1652?

1426 → (4 minutes) 1430 → (2 hours) 1630 → (22 minutes) 1652

Remember that there are 60 minutes in 1 hour.

Total time = 2 hours 26 minutes

Timetables

Timetables often use 24-hour clock times. Timetables should be read carefully.

Example

The timetable illustrates the tram times from Bury to Manchester.

If the timetable is written in 24-hour clock time, make sure your answers are in 24-hour clock times.

Bury	0012	0036	Every 30	0706	0711	Every 5	0906
Whitefield	0020	0044	minutes	0714	0719	minutes	0914
Bowker Vale	0025	0049	until	0719	0724	until	0919
Manchester	0029	0053		0723	0728		0923

The 0025 tram from Bowker Vale

0706 tram from Bury arrives in Manchester at 0723

There will be a tram from Bury every 5 minutes from 0711 until 0906, i.e. 0716, 0721, . . .

(a) Leroy sets off from Bury at 0036. How long does it take him to get to Manchester?

(b) What time is the next tram from Bury after the 0036 one?

(c) Diana arrives at Whitefield station at 0740. What is the time of the next tram to Manchester?

(a) 0036 departs Bury → 0053 arrives Manchester   Time = 17 minutes.

Beware! Do not write 0066. There are only 60 minutes in 1 hour.

(b) Next tram is at 0106, i.e. 0036 + 30 minutes

(c) Trams run every 5 minutes, i.e. 0719, 0724, 0729, 0734, 0739, 0744.

Diana arrives at 0740, so her next tram is the 0744 one.

Compound measures

Speed

Speed can be measured in kilometres per hour (km/h), miles per hour (m.p.h.) and metres per second (m/s).

km/h, m/s and m.p.h. are all **compound measures** because they involve a combination of basic measures.

Just remember the letters – it's quicker.

The formula for **average speed** is

$$\text{average speed} = \frac{\text{total distance travelled}}{\text{total time taken}} \quad \text{or} \quad s = \frac{d}{t}$$

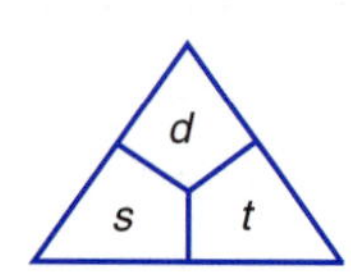

From the speed formula two other formulae can be found.

$$\text{time} = \frac{\text{distance}}{\text{speed}} \quad \text{or} \quad t = \frac{d}{s}$$

This triangle can be used to help you remember the formulae.

$$\text{distance} = \text{speed} \times \text{time} \quad \text{or} \quad d = s \times t$$

Example

Bronwen walks 5 km in 2 hours. Find her average speed.

Since the distance is in kilometres and time is in hours, speed is in km/h.

$$s = \frac{d}{t} = \frac{5}{2} = 2.5 \text{ km/h}$$

Example

Joanne drove 200 miles in 4 hours 30 minutes. At what average speed did she travel?

$$s = \frac{d}{t} = \frac{200}{4.5} = 44.\dot{4} \text{ m.p.h.}$$

Remember 30 minutes = $\frac{30}{60}$ hour = 0.5 hours.

Example

Liam drove 90 miles at an average speed of 60 m.p.h. How long did it take him?

$$t = \frac{d}{s} = \frac{90}{60} = 1.5 \text{ hours}$$

time = 1 hour 30 minutes

0.5 × 60 minutes = 30 minutes.

Example

How far does Giovanni walk if he walks at a speed of 4 miles per hour for 5 hours 30 minutes?

$d = s \times t = 4 \times 5.5$

distance = 22 miles

Solving numerical problems Questions

1. What does a display of [4.6] mean, if the calculation was in pounds and pence?
2. By trial and improvement, find correct to 1 decimal place the value of x where $x^3 = 25$.
3. John worked out 106 × 52 and obtained the answer 55 120. By estimating the answer to the calculation, say whether John's answer is to the right order of magnitude.
4. Philip works a 38-hour week at £4.26 per hour. He works an additional 3 hours at time and a half and 4 hours at double time. What is his final wage at the end of the week?
5. Penny has £4 250 in the bank. If the interest rate is 6.8% p.a. how much interest on her savings will she get at the end of the year?
6. A telephone bill is for £69.42. VAT at $17\frac{1}{2}$% is added on. What is the bill's total, including VAT?
7. A car costs £7 295. If a deposit of 20% is paid and 24 monthly instalments of £250, what is the final bill for the car?
8. The exchange rate is 7.50 French francs to the pound. If I have £320, how many French francs will I receive?
9. Beryl walks 18 km in 4 hours. What is her average speed?
10. It is 4:35 p.m. Write this as a 24-hour clock time.

Functional relationships

Using letters

Examiner's tips and your notes

In **algebra**, letters are used to represent numbers.

Example

Lucy has some sweets, Jason has 4 less than Lucy.
Write this information with letters.

Let p be the number of sweets Lucy has.

Jason has 4 less than Lucy. This is written as

$p - 4$

This is known as an **expression.**

Example

In a game John has r counters. Write down the number of counters each person has using r.

(a) Carol has twice as many as John. Carol has $2 \times r = 2r$.

(b) Vali has 12 less than John. Vali has $r - 12$.

(c) Stuart has half as many as John. Stuart has $r \div 2 = \frac{r}{2}$.

(d) Hilary has 5 less than Carol. Hilary has $2r - 5$.

In algebra, the × sign is missed out.

In algebra, divisions are often written as one expression over the other.

Substitution

Replacing the letters with a number is known as **substitution**.

When substituting:

- write out the expression first and then replace the letters with the values given;
- use your calculator where possible and pay attention to **order of operations**;
- avoid silly answers by using **estimation** as a rough check.

Examples

Using $a = 2$, $b = 6.1$, $c = -3$, $d = 4$, find the values of these expressions:

(a) $\frac{a + b}{2}$ (b) $a^2 + d^2$ (c) $\frac{2d}{3}$ (d) ab

It is important that you have a calculator that you are used to for the examination.

Remember to show the substitution, like this:

(a) $\frac{a + b}{2} = \frac{2 + 6.1}{2} = \frac{8.1}{2} = 4.05$

(b) $a^2 + d^2 = 2^2 + 4^2 = 4 + 16 = 20$

(c) $\frac{2d}{3} = \frac{2 \times 4}{3} = \frac{8}{3} = 2.\dot{6}$

(d) $ab = a \times b = 2 \times 6.1 = 12.2$

Remember: a^2 means a × a.

ab just means a × b.

Make sure that you show each step in your working out.

Example

If $U = 4$ and $V = 3$, find the values of these expressions:

(a) $3U + 2V$ (b) $2 \times (U + V)$

(a) $3U + 2V = (3 \times 4) + (2 \times 3) = 12 + 6 = 18$

(b) $2 \times (U + V) = 2 \times (4 + 3) = 2 \times (7) = 14$

Remember: brackets need to be worked out first.

Number patterns and sequences

A **sequence** is a list of numbers. There is usually a relationship between the numbers.

Each value in the sequence is called a **term**.

There are lots of different number patterns. Here are just a few.

When finding a missing number in the number pattern it is sensible to see what's happening in the gaps.

The gap between the numbers is the same each time.

Examples

1 3 5 7 9

+2 +2 +2 +2

The rule for this pattern is **add 2 each time**.

It is important to put the words **each time** when describing these number patterns.

12 8 4 0 −4

−4 −4 −4 −4

The rule for this pattern is **subtract 4 each time**.

Write the change in the gap.

2 5 10 17 26

+3 +5 +7 +9

The rule for this pattern is **add the next odd number each time**.

When asked to describe a rule, try to make it clear.

2 6 18 24

× 3 × 3 × 3

The rule is **multiply by 3 each time**.

128 64 32 16 8 4

÷ 2 ÷ 2 ÷ 2 ÷ 2 ÷ 2

The rule is **divide by 2 each time**.

1 1 2 3 5 8 13

1 + 1 1 + 2 2 + 3 3 + 5 5 + 8

This is called the **Fibonacci sequence.**

The rule is **add the previous two numbers each time**.

Common number patterns

You must learn these number patterns and be able to recognise them.

Square numbers	1	4	9	16	25, . . .
Cube numbers	1	8	27	64	125, . . .
Triangular numbers	1	3	6	10	15, . . .

Finding the *n*th term of a linear sequence

The *n*th term is often denoted by U_n. For example, the 12th term is written as U_{12}.

For a **linear sequence**, the *n*th term takes the form $U_n = an + b$.

Example

Find the *n*th term of this sequence: 1, 3, 5, 7, 9 . . .

Rewrite the pattern next to the term numbers.

This is U_1, the first term

Term number	1	2	3	4	5 . . .	*n*
Pattern	1	3	5	7	9	
Difference	2	2	2	2		

The gap (or difference) gives the value of a; here a = 2.

$U_n = an + b$

$U_n = 2n + b$ Replace *a* with the value 2.

$1 = 2 \times 1 + b$ Try out the rule with the first term U_1. $n = 1$ and $U_1 = 1$.

Practise on lots of sequences. Finding nth terms is hard.

$1 - 2 = b$ Adjust the rule to find *b*.

$b = -1$ So $U_n = 2n - 1$

Example

Find the *n*th term of this sequence: 4, 7, 10, 13.

Term number	1	2	3	4 . . .	*n*
Pattern	4	7	10	13 . . .	
Difference	3	3	3		

$U_n = an + b$

$U_n = 3n + b$ Replace *a* with 3 (the difference).

$4 = 3 \times 1 + b$ Replace U_n with 4 and *n* with 1 (the first term).

$4 = 3 + b$

$b = 1$ Adjust the rule to find *b*.

So $U_n = 3n + 1$

Check If $n = 2$, $U_2 = 3 \times 2 + 1 = 7$

The second term in the pattern is 7, so the rule for the *n*th term works here.

When you have found the nth term always check it works.

Coordinates

Coordinates are used to describe the position of a point.

When reading coordinates, the number of units **across** is read **first**, and the number of units **up or down** is read **second**.

Coordinates are always put in **brackets** with a **comma** in between, as in (2, 3).

The **x-axis** is the across (**horizontal**) axis. The **y-axis** is the up (**vertical**) axis.

The point where the x and y axes meet is called the **origin**.

Remember the comma and the brackets.

Example

P has the coordinates (4, 3).

R has the coordinates (–2, –5).

S has the coordinates (0, 4).

T has the coordinates (3, –4).

U has the coordinates (–3, 2).

V has the coordinates (–4.5, 3.5).

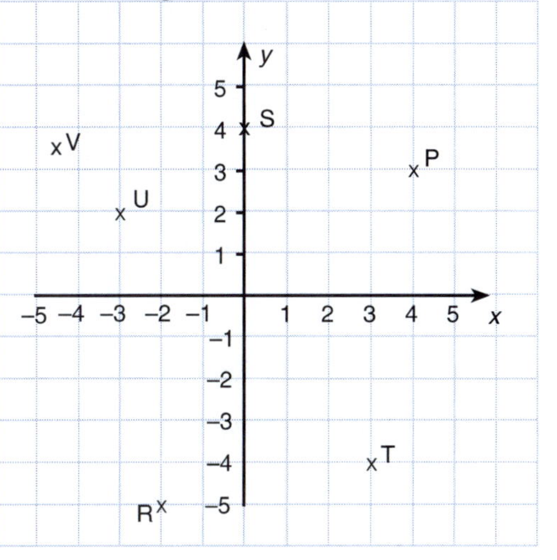

Function machines

Example

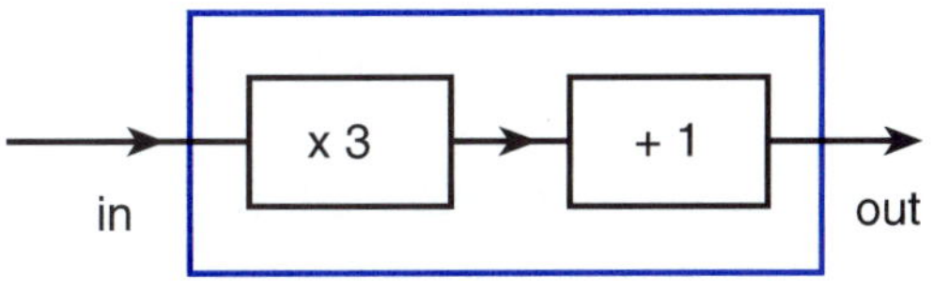

When the numbers are fed into this function machine, they are first multiplied by 3 and then added to 1.

If 1 is fed in, 4 comes out (i.e. $1 \times 3 + 1 = 4$).

If 2 is fed in, 7 comes out (i.e. $2 \times 3 + 1 = 7$).

If 3 is fed in, 10 comes out (i.e. $3 \times 3 + 1 = 10$).

If 4 is fed in, 13 comes out (i.e. $4 \times 3 + 1 = 13$).

This transformation can be illustrated with a **mapping diagram**, like this:

$1 \rightarrow 4$

$2 \rightarrow 7$

$3 \rightarrow 10$

$4 \rightarrow 13$

To describe the mapping, $x \rightarrow 3x + 1$ is written. This is read 'x becomes 3x + 1.'

Graph drawing

Coordinates and function machines are used to draw graphs.

You will be asked to draw two types of graphs.

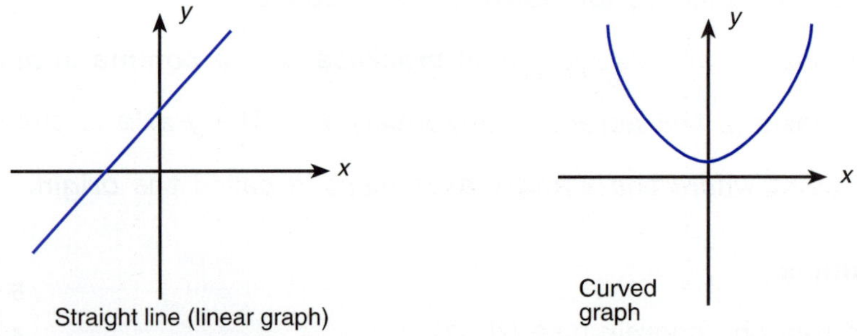

Graphs of the form $y = mx + c$

These are straight line (**linear**) graphs.

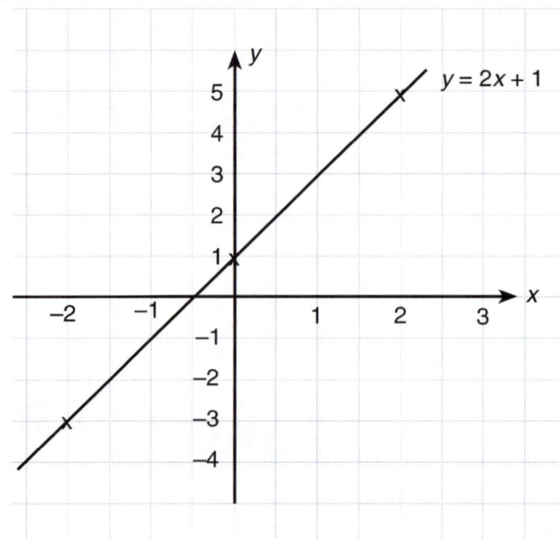

Example

Draw the graph of $y = 2x + 1$.

- Choose some values of x, for example –2, 0, 2.
- Replace x in the equation with each value.

If your points do not form a straight line, go back and check them.

$x = -2,\quad y = 2 \times -2 + 1 = -3$

$x = 0,\quad y = 2 \times 0 + 1 = 1$

$x = 2,\quad y = 2 \times 2 + 1 = 5$

x	–2	0	2
y	–3	1	5

- Plot the coordinates (–2, –3), (0, 1), (2, 5). Join them to give a straight line.
- Label the line once it is drawn.

Example

Complete the mapping diagram for $x \rightarrow 3x - 2$.

Complete the coordinates shown.

Use your calculator to help you work out the coordinates.

x	→	3x – 2	(x, y)
–2	→	–8	(–2, –8)
–1	→	–5	(–1, –5)
0	→	–2	(0, –2)
1	→	1	(1, 1)
2	→	4	(2, 4)
3	→	7	(3, 7)

Plot the coordinates, then join them up with a straight line.

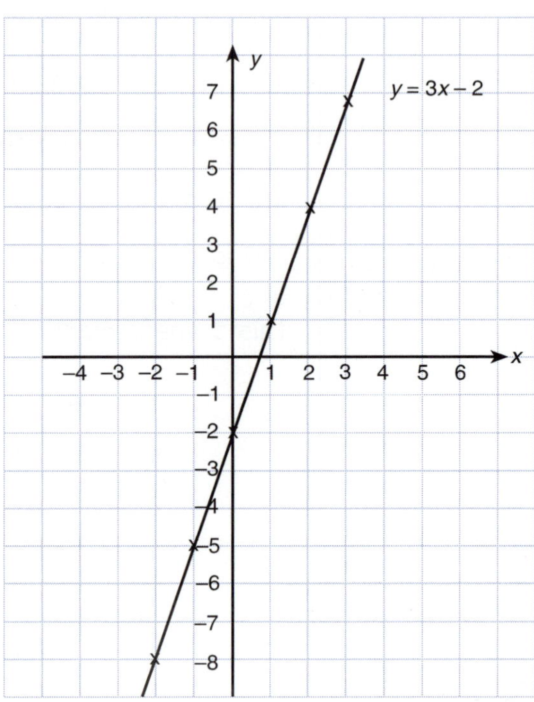

Graphs of the form $y = a$, $x = b$

Example

Draw the line $y = 4$.

Example

Draw the line $x = 2$.

$y = a$ is a **horizontal** line with every y coordinate equal to a.
$x = b$ is a **vertical** line with every x coordinate equal to b

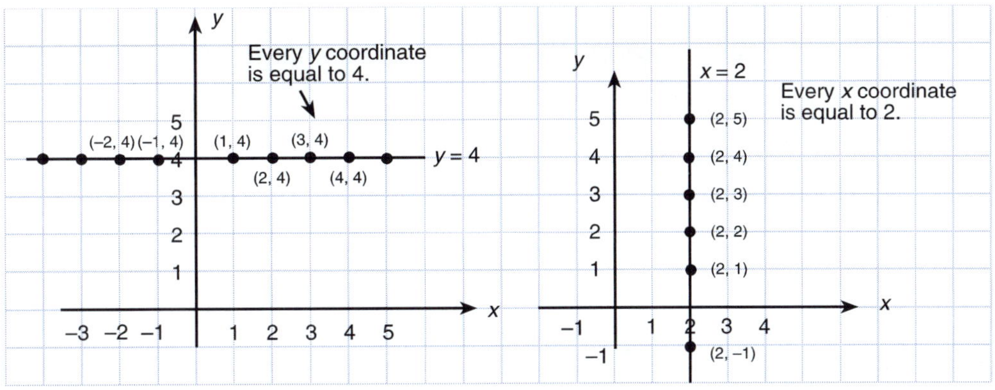

Graphs of the form $y = x^2 + a$

Remember x^2 means $x \times x$.

These graphs are curved.

Example

Draw the graph of $y = x^2 - 1$.

To work out the y coordinates just replace x with different values.

- Work out the y coordinates in a table.

Use a calculator to help you work out the coordinates.

x	−3	−2	−1	0	1	2	3
y	8	3	0	−1	0	3	8

$-3^2 - 1 = 9 - 1 = 8$ (Remember: -3^2 means $-3 \times -3 = 9$).

- These give the coordinates of the curve. The curve can now be plotted.

Draw a smooth curve through all the points.

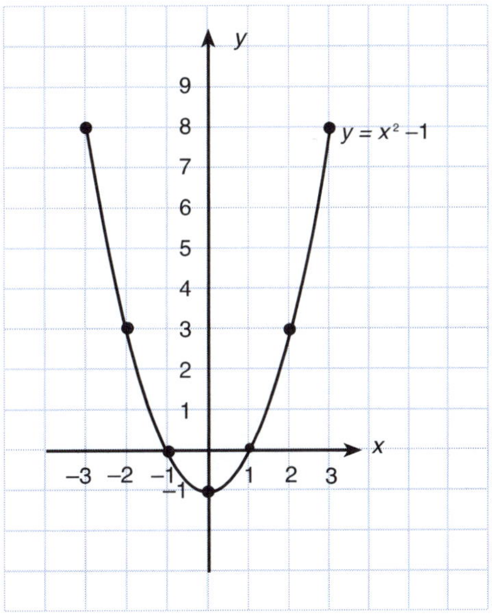

- Join up the points with a smooth curve and label the graph.

Using linear graphs

Linear graphs are often used to show relationships.

Example

Neville has a window cleaning round. He charges £5 for the use of materials and £1 per hour after that. This information can be put into a table.

Number of hours worked	0	1	2	3	4	5
Cost in £	5	6	7	8	9	10

Even though Neville has not cleaned any window, he charges £5 for the use of the materials.

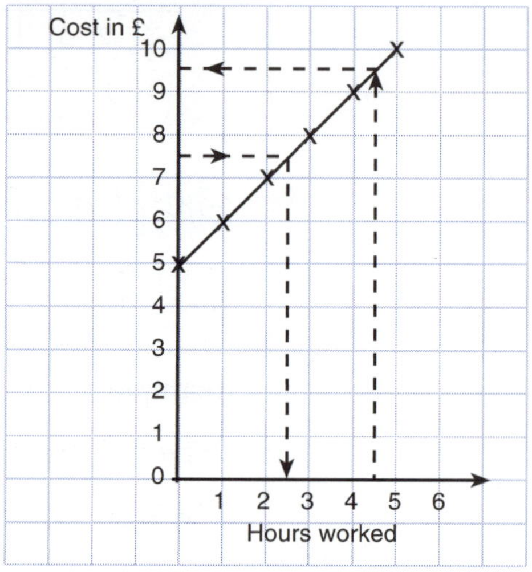

Notice that the graph gives a straight line.

The graph can be used to find, for example, how long Neville works if he charges £7.50 ($2\frac{1}{2}$ hours) and what he charges if he works $4\frac{1}{2}$ hours (£9.50).

Conversion graphs

These are used to convert one measurement into another measurement; for example, litres to pints, km to miles, £ to dollars etc.

Draw lines on the graph to show how you obtain your answers.

Example

Suppose £1 is worth $1.50. Draw a conversion graph.

£	1	2	3	4	5
$	1.5	3.0	4.5	6.0	7.5

× 1.5

- Make a table of values.
- Plot each of these points on the graph paper.
- To change dollars to £, read across to the line then read down; for example, $4 is £2.67 (approx.).
- To change £ to dollars, read up to the line then read across; for example, £4.50 is $6.80 (approx.).

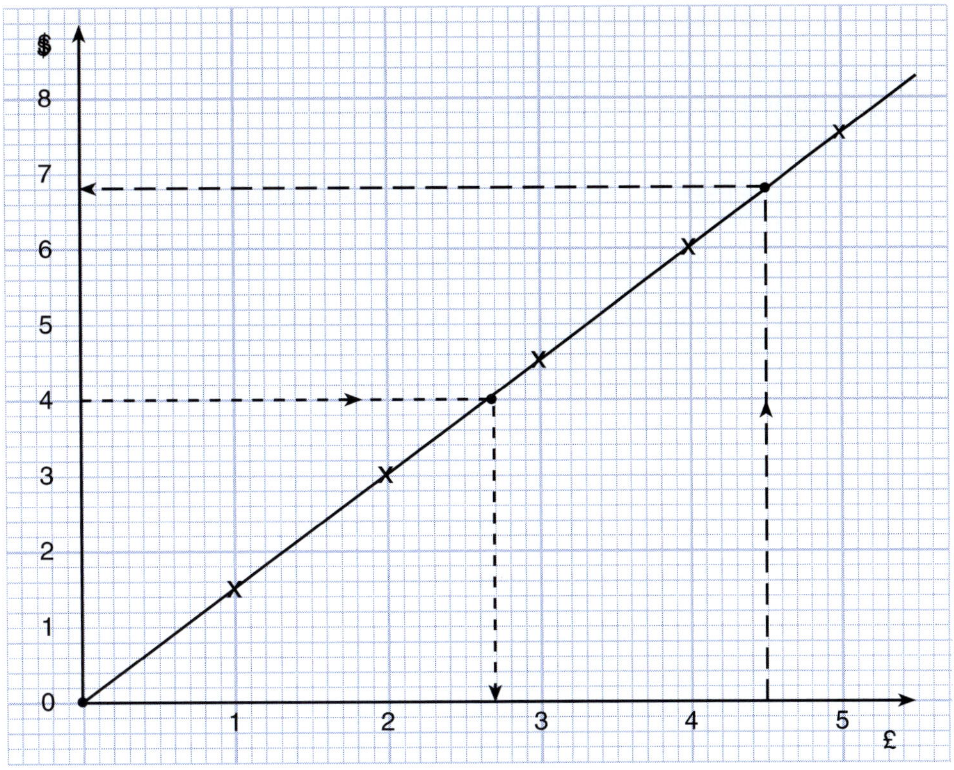

Distance–time graphs

These are often known as **travel graphs**.

Distance is on the vertical axis; time is on the horizontal axis.

The speed of an object can be found from a distance–time graph by using:

$$\text{speed} = \frac{\text{distance travelled}}{\text{time taken}}$$

Example

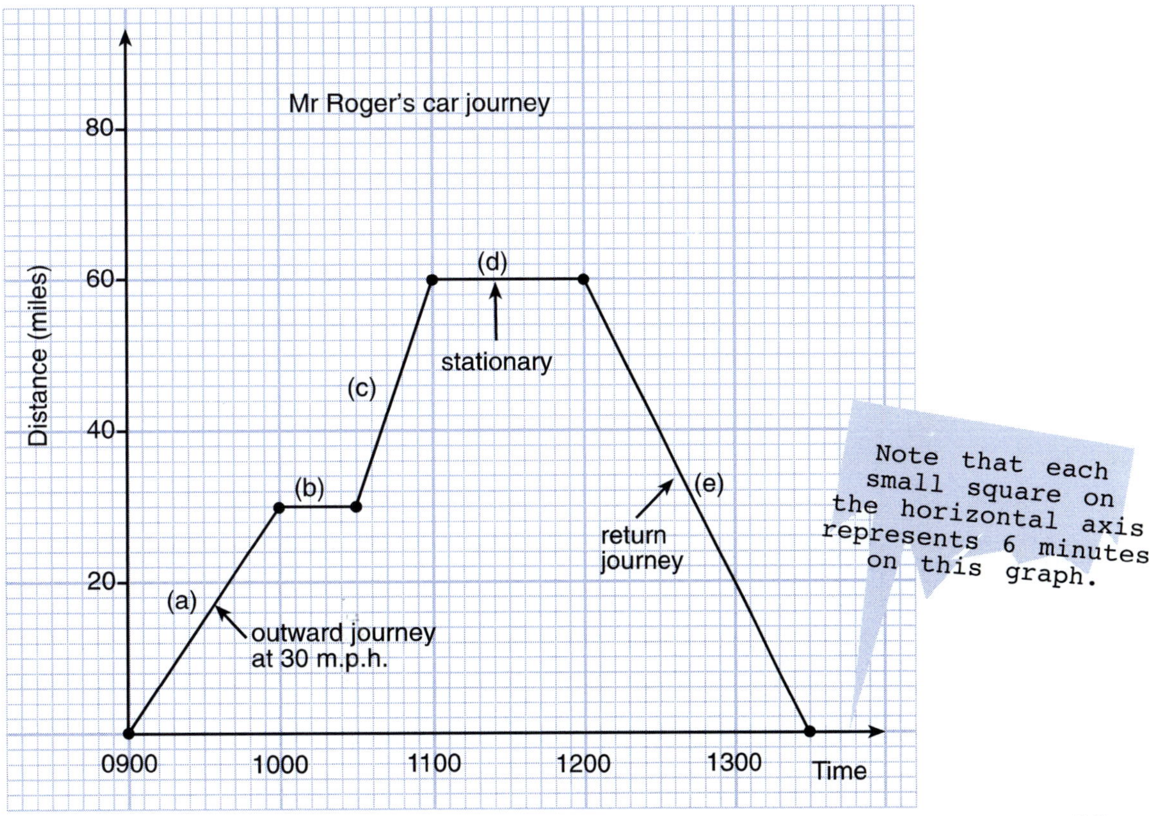

The graph shows Mr Roger's car journey. Work out his speed at each stage of the journey.

(a) For the first stage of the journey

$$\text{speed} = \frac{\text{distance}}{\text{time}} = \frac{30}{1} = 30 \text{ m.p.h.}$$

So the car travels at 30 m.p.h. for 1 hour.

(b) The car is stationary for 30 minutes.

(c) The graph is steeper so the car is travelling faster.

$$\text{speed} = \frac{\text{distance}}{\text{time}} = \frac{30}{0.5} = 60 \text{ m.p.h.}$$

(d) The car is stationary for 1 hour.

(e) For the return journey the speed is

$$\text{speed} = \frac{\text{distance}}{\text{time}} = \frac{60}{1.5} = 40 \text{ m.p.h.}$$

Always check you understand the graph's scales before starting a question.

Remember 30 minutes is 0.5 hours.

Questions

1 Write these expressions as simply as possible.

(a) 8 less than b (b) 12 more than x (c) 5 less than 2 lots of p

(d) h divided by 4 (e) p less than 6 (f) h less than 3 lots of x

2 If $y = 3$, work out $4y + 2$.

3 If $a = 6$, $b = 4.1$ and $c = -3$, work out:

(a) $2a + b$ (b) $3a - 2$ (c) $2c + 6a$ (d) $\frac{b^2}{2}$ (e) ab

4 Write down the next number in the sequence and describe the rule.

(a) 5, 7, 9, 11, . . . (b) 9, 6, 3, 0, . . .

(c) 5, 10, 20, 40, . . . (d) 81, 27, 9, 3, . . .

(e) 6, 6, 12, 18, 30, . . . (f) 1, 4, 9, 16, . . .

5 Find the nth term (U_n) of these sequences:

(a)

Term	1	2	3 . . .	n
Sequence	5	9	13 . . .	

(b)

Term	1	2	3 . . .	n
Sequence	6	8	10 . . .	

6 Complete the two tables below and draw the graphs using a grid as shown.

(a) $y = 2x + 3$

x	−3	−2	−1	0	1	2	3
y		−1			5		9

(b) $y = x^2 + 2$

x	−3	−2	−1	0	1	2	3
y	11		3	2		6	

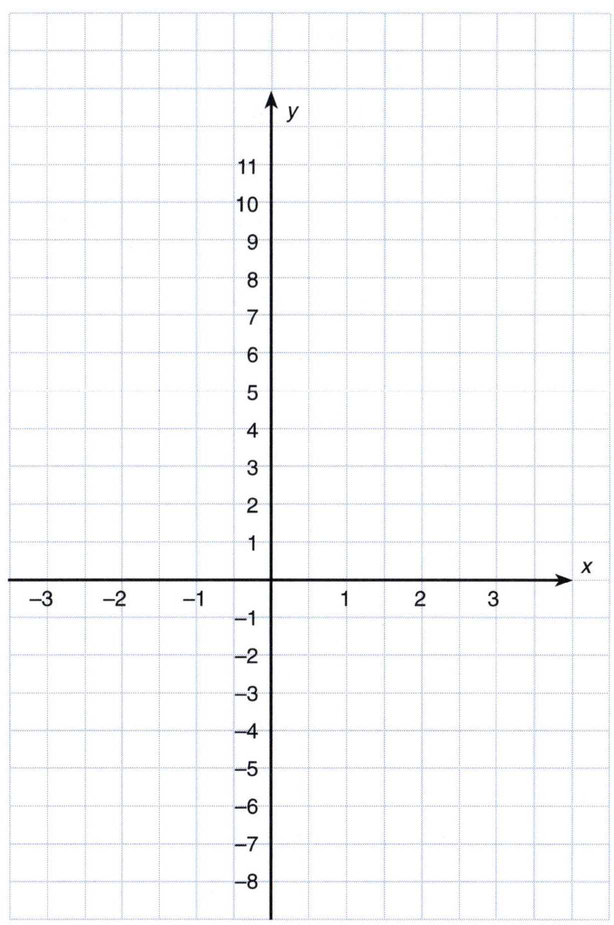

Equations and formulae

Algebraic conventions

Examiner's tips and your notes

There are several rules to follow when writing algebraic expressions.

- $a + a + a = 3$ lots of a or $3a$
- $3 \times a = 3a$ In algebra the multiplication sign is missed out.
- $a \times a = a^2$, **not** $2a$
- $a \times a \times a = a^3$, **not** $3a$
- $a \times b \times 2 = 2ab$ The number is put first and then the letters are in alphabetical order, there are no multiplication signs. For example, $a \times 6 \times b \times y \times c = 6abcy$.
- Divisions in algebra are usually written as fractions, for example $\frac{r}{2}$.
- $a \times a \times 2 = 2a^2$, **not** $(2a)^2$

Writing simple formulae

$p + 3$ is an **expression**.

$y = p + 3$ is a **formula**, since it has an equals sign (=) in it.

Example

There are 10 chairs in a row. How many chairs are there in:

(a) 4 rows, (b) x rows?

(a) $4 \times 10 = 40$ chairs (b) $x \times 10 = 10x$ chairs.

x can take any value.

In words, the rule for the number of chairs could be written as

number of chairs = 10 × number of rows.

This is a **formula** for working out the number of chairs in any rows. If c represents number of chairs and r represents the number of rows,

$c = 10 \times r$ or $c = 10r$

This formula is in **symbol** form.

Example

Bonnie hires a van. There is a standing charge of £8 and then it costs £3 per hour. How much does it cost for

(a) 6 hours' hire, (b) y hours' hire? (c) Write a formula for the cost C.

(a) $8 + (3 \times 6) = £26$

(b) $8 + (3 \times y) = 8 + 3y$

(c) $C = 8 + 3y$ This is a formula for working out the cost of hiring the van for y hours, where y can take any value.

Make sure you include an = sign in your formula.

Example

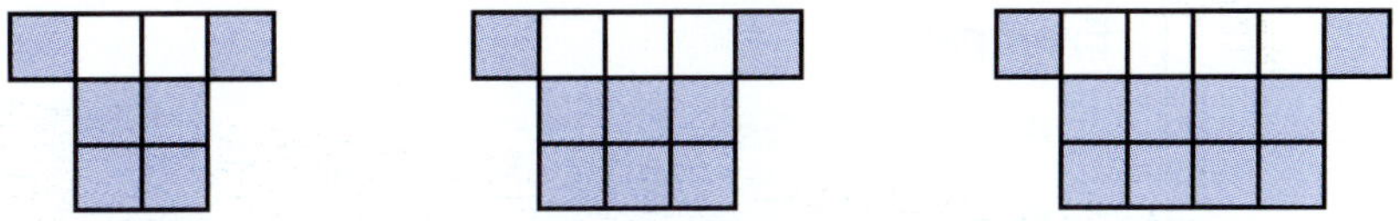

The diagrams show some patterns using grey and white paving slabs.

(a) If there are 6 white paving slabs, how many grey ones are there?

(b) Write a formula for the number of grey paving slabs (G) in a pattern that uses W white ones.

(a) Drawing the diagram:

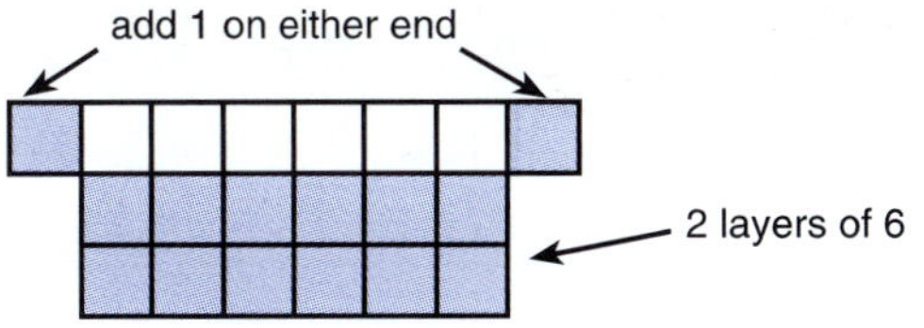

So 14 grey paving slabs are needed.

Check that your formula works by trying a simple example.

(b) $G = W \times 2 + 2$ or $G = 2W + 2$

2W represents the 2 layers. + 2 gives the grey tiles which are on either end of the white tiles.

Substituting values into formulae

This is the same as substituting values into expressions. Simply replace the letters with the values.

Example

$P = 2 \times (l + w)$. Work out the value of P if $l = 4.9$ and $w = 10$.

$P = 2 \times (4.9 + 10)$
$= 2 \times (14.9)$
$= 29.8$

Work out the brackets first.

Show the substitution and full working out.

Example

The formula $F = \frac{9}{5}C + 32$ is used to change temperatures in degrees centigrade (C) to temperatures in degrees fahrenheit (F). If $C = 26$, work out the value of F.

$F = \frac{9}{5}C + 32$
$= \frac{9}{5} \times 26 + 32$
$= 78.8$

Substitute C = 26 into the formula. Note $\frac{9}{5}$C means $\frac{9}{5} \times$ C.

Work this out carefully on your calculator.

Simplifying formulae

Collecting like terms

Expressions can be simplified by **collecting like terms**. Only collect the terms if their letters and powers are **identical**.

Examples

$4a + 2a = 6a$

$9a + 3b$ cannot be simplified since there are no like terms.

$3b + 4b - b = 6b$

Note that b means 1b.

$4a + 3b + 2a - b$ Rewrite with the 'a's together and the 'b's together.
$= 4a + 2a + 3b - b$
$= 6a + 2b$

Remember to put the sign between the 2a and 2b.

$12a - 4b + 2b - 10a = 2a - 2b$

This minus sign is part of the term 4b.

Multiplying letters and numbers

Algebraic expressions are often simplified by multiplying them together. When multiplying expressions, multiply the numbers together, then multiply the letters together.

multiply the numbers.

multiply the letters.

Examples

(a) $5a \times 2b = 5 \times 2 \times a \times b = 10ab$

(b) $2a \times 4b \times 3c = 2 \times 4 \times 3 \times a \times b \times c = 24abc$

(c) $5a \times 2a = 5 \times 2 \times a \times a = 10a^2$

(d) $6a \times 3a \times 2a = 6 \times 3 \times 2 \times a \times a \times a = 36a^3$

Remember $a \times a = a^2$ (a squared) and $a \times a \times a = a^3$ (a cubed).

Multiplying out brackets

This helps to simplify algebraic expressions. Everything inside the bracket is multiplied by everything outside the bracket.

Examples

This is known as **expanding** the brackets.

$3(a + b) = 3 \times a + 3 \times b = 3a + 3b$

The multiplication sign is not shown here.

$5(y + 2) = 5 \times y + 5 \times 2 = 5y + 10$

$a(b + c) = a \times b + a \times c = ab + ac$

$r(2r + 3y) = r \times 2r + r \times 3y = 2r^2 + 3ry$

Remember that $r \times r = r^2$ and $r \times 3y$ is written with the number first, as 3ry.

If the term outside the bracket is **negative**, all of the signs of the terms inside the bracket are **changed** when multiplying out.

Examples

$-4\,(2x + 3) = -4 \times 2x + -4 \times 3 = -8x - 12$

Remember
Like signs give a '+'.
So 2 × 1 = 2 and −2 × −1 = 2.
Unlike signs give a '−'.
So 2 × −1 = −2 and −2 × 1 = −2.

Take care when multiplying with negative numbers. Try to remember the rules.

$-2\,(a - b) = -2 \times a + -2 \times -b = -2a + 2b$

$-(a + b) = -1 \times a + -1 \times b = -a - b$

−(a + b) really means −1 × (a + b).

To simplify expressions:

- expand the brackets first;
- then collect like terms.

Example

Expand and simplify $2(x - 1) + 3(x + 2)$.

$2(x - 1) + 3(x + 2)$	Multiply out the brackets.
$= 2x - 2 + 3x + 6$	Collect like terms.
$= 5x + 4$	

Example

Be very careful when multiplying by negative numbers.

Expand and simplify $5a + 2b - 3(a - b)$.

$5a + 2b - 3(a - b)$	Multiply out the brackets.
$= 5a + 2b - 3a + 3b$	Collect like terms.
$= 2a + 5b$	

Inequalities

These are expressions where one side is **not equal** to the other.

$<$ 'is less than'.

$\leq$ 'is less than or equal to'.

$>$ 'is greater than'.

$\geq$ 'is greater than or equal to'.

Examples

$-6 < 10$ $\quad 5 > 3$

$x \geq 6$ means x is any value greater than or equal to 6; for example 6, 7, 8, 9, . . .

$x < 2$ means x is any value less than 2 for example 1, 0, −1, . . .

Equations

An equation involves an unknown value which has to be worked out.

The **balance** method is usually used. In this, whatever is done to one side of the equation must be done to the other.

'Solve' just means 'work out'.

Examples

Solve: (a) $n - 5 = 20$ (b) $n + 6 = 10$ (c) $3x = 21$ (d) $\frac{x}{6} = 4$

(a) $n - 5 = 20$ Add 5 to both sides.
$n = 20 + 5$
$n = 25$

(b) $n + 6 = 10$ Subtract 6 from both sides.
$n = 10 - 6$
$n = 4$

(c) $3x = 21$ Divide both sides by 3.
$x = \frac{21}{3}$
$x = 7$

(d) $\frac{x}{6} = 4$ Multiply both sides by 6.
$x = 6 \times 4$
$x = 24$

Equations which combine operations

Examples

Solve $\frac{x}{2} - 3 = 2$

$\frac{x}{2} = 2 + 3$ Add 3 to both sides.
$\frac{x}{2} = 5$
$x = 5 \times 2$ Multiply both sides by 2.
$x = 10$

Solve $3x + 7 = 1$

The solution to an equation can be positive or negative and it may be a fraction or decimal.

$3x = 1 - 7$ Subtract 7 from both sides.
$3x = -6$
$x = \frac{-6}{3}$ Divide both sides by 3.
$x = -2$

Equations with brackets

When an equation has a bracket, the bracket needs to be multiplied out first.

Examples

Solve $4(2x + 3) = 24$

$8x + 12 = 24$	Multiply out the brackets.
$8x = 24 - 12$	Subtract 12 from both sides.
$8x = 12$	
$x = \frac{12}{8} = 1\frac{1}{2}$	

Solve $3(2x - 1) = 21$

$6x - 3 = 21$	Multiply out the brackets.
$6x = 21 + 3$	Add 3 to both sides.
$6x = 24$	
$x = 4$	

Equations with unknowns on both sides

When there are letters on both sides, it is best to keep the letter on the side with the most.

Example

Solve $5n + 2 = 3n + 8$

Take care with the signs of the values and show each step in your working.

$5n - 3n + 2 = 8$	Subtract $3n$ from both sides.
$2n + 2 = 8$	
$2n = 8 - 2$	Subtract 2 from both sides.
$2n = 6$	
$n = \frac{6}{2}$	Divide both sides by 2.
$n = 3$	

Example

Solve $3(2a + 1) = 2(a + 2)$

You must first get rid of the brackets then sort out as normal.

$6a + 3 = 2a + 4$	Multiply out the brackets first.
$6a - 2a + 3 = 4$	
$4a + 3 = 4$	
$4a = 4 - 3$	
$4a = 1$	
$a = \frac{1}{4}$	

Using equations to solve problems

Example

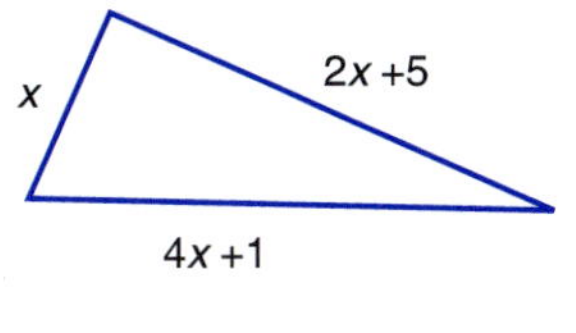

The perimeter of the triangle is 20 cm. Work out the value of x and hence find the lengths of the three sides.

$x + 2x + 5 + 4x + 1 = 20$

The perimeter is found by adding the lengths together. Collect like terms. Solve the equation as before.

$7x + 6 = 20$
$7x = 20 - 6$
$7x = 14$
$x = \frac{14}{7}$
$x = 2$

Remember to check that you have answered the question.

So the lengths of the sides are 2 (= x), 9 (= $4x + 1$) and 9 (= $2x + 5$).

Equations and formulae

Questions

1 For the hire of a coach there is a standing charge of £175, plus a further £6 per person on the coach.

(a) Work out total cost if there are 9 people on the coach.

(b) Work out total cost if there are 50 people on the coach.

(c) Write a formula for the cost c, if there are p people on the coach.

2 If Jiffy bags cost 35p each, how much would m bags cost?

3 $y = 4c + 2d$, where $c = 6.9$ and $d = 2.4$. Work out y.

4 Simplify these expressions.

(a) $5a + 2a$ (b) $6c + 2c - c$ (c) $2a + 3b - b + 4a$

(d) $4 \times 2b$ (e) $7a \times 3b$ (f) $2a \times 5a^2$

5 Multiply out these brackets.

(a) $2(x + 4)$ (b) $5(2y - 3)$ (c) $a(a + b)$ (d) $2a(a - c)$

6 Solve these equations.

(a) $n + 6 = 8$ (b) $p - 9 = 10$

(c) $2a = 20$ (d) $\frac{n}{5} = 6$

(e) $5x - 2 = 8$ (f) $6n + 4 = 22$

(g) $5y + 2 = 3y + 6$ (h) $9y - 3 = 2y + 18$

(i) $2(x + 4) = 10$

7

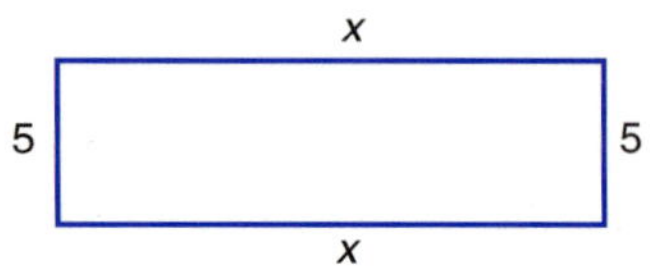

The perimeter of this rectangle is 30 cm. Work out the length x.

GCSE Success with Letts Educational

FREE Revision Planner overleaf

Save £5 when you purchase Revise GCSE and a GCSE Q&A

Revise GCSE

The UK's best selling study guides, provide all you need for exam success! Each guide offers complete study and reference support throughout your GCSE Course. We're so sure of this series it even comes with a 'success or your money back' guarantee.

Questions and Answers

Practice, Practice, Practice ... that's the secret to GCSE success. Examiners say that practice really does improve your GCSE grade.

The Letts Question and Answers series provides

- Questions specifically written by examiners for their relevance to the year 2000 exams
- Full Answers to every question with step-by-step explanations
- Examiner's tips to achieve maximum marks and avoid common mistakes

This series is crucial for improving your exam technique and performance

Revise GCSE in a Week

The ultimate series to help you in the crucial week before your exams begin DON'T PANIC – in one week or less this book will

- Give you the information that you really need; and no more
- Make sure the essentials really sink in
- Provide a timed revision programme to keep you on course

Created by the staff of one of the UK's most successful tutorial colleges, this one-week crammer course gives you the inside knowledge for GCSE success – the ideal refresher course to reinforce your revision

Save £2 when you purchase a GCSE in a Week or a GCSE Passcards

GCSE Passcards

Concise revision notes especially prepared by examiners, giving you security in the knowledge that you are learning the essentials. With a clear Lay-out using summary lists and key points, Passcards are the ideal quick revision tool.

Grade A Secrets

The ultimate mock exams.

GCSE examiners have written these papers in the same style and format as the GCSE exams.

Each pack contains

- Examiners report on what 1999 students did wrong and how to get it right
- Examiners analysis of what is likely to come up in this years exams

Special Offers – save £££££££s

Order any GCSE in a week and Passcards and save £2

Order any Revise GCSE and Questions and Answers and save £5

To order see the back page

Letts GCSE Year Pla

This revision planner is designed for you to pull out and use. It will help you prepare well and organise your revision – as well as boosting your confidence and your grades! Stick the planner on your wall and mark on key dates in your revision programme.

We hav
- Term
- Mock
- Your

Your future starts here

1999

September

Start of your final GCSE Year

Make your life easier – and avoid stress and panic later on – start preparing for your GCSEs NOW!

October

Coursework is important

Understand and learn your coursework thoroughly – it can count for 20-60% of your final mark.

November

Start revising for mock exams

Take your mock exams seriously – they test your knowledge, and give you important practice in answering exam questions.

December

Mock Exams

Get the most from your mocks. Improve your exam technique:
- read the questions carefully
- underline key words in the questions
- allocate your time according to marks
- answer the question asked!

2000

January

Learn from your mocks

Mock exams can help you and your teachers assess your progress. Use your mock results check that you have all the information and revision aids that you need for the rest of the year.

	September	October	November	December	January
Monday			1		
Tuesday			2		
Wednesday	1		3	1	
Thursday	2		4	2	
Friday	3	1	5	3	
Saturday	4	2	6	4	1
Sunday	5	3	7	5	2
Monday	6	4	8	6	3
Tuesday	7	5	9	7	4
Wednesday	8	6	10	8	5
Thursday	9	7	11	9	6
Friday	10	8	12	10	7
Saturday	11	9	13	11	8
Sunday	12	10	14	12	9
Monday	13	11	15	13	10
Tuesday	14	12	16	14	11
Wednesday	15	13	17	15	12
Thursday	16	14	18	16	13
Friday	17	15	19	17	14
Saturday	18	16	20	18	15
Sunday	19	17	21	19	16
Monday	20	18	22	20	17
Tuesday	21	19	23	21	18
Wednesday	22	20	24	22	19
Thursday	23	21	25	23	20
Friday	24	22	26	24	21
Saturday	25	23	27	25	22
Sunday	26	24	28	26	23
Monday	27	25	29	27	24
Tuesday	28	26	30	28	25
Wednesday	29	27		29	26
Thursday	30	28		30	27
Friday		29		31	28
Saturday		30			29
Sunday		31			30
Monday					31

GCSE Exam

nner

icated key dates in the revision calendar, but you might want to mark on:

- s and holidays
- m dates
- E exam timetable
- Coursework deadlines
- An outline revision plan

February

et busy – only 4 nonths to go to our GCSEs

lanning your work neans that you are more kely to revise properly it will also help you tay cool and avoid tress.

it. the e

March

Make a plan

Prepare your revision plan. Make sure you fill in all your commitments including:

- lesson times
- school activities
- other activities (part-time jobs etc)
- time for relaxation and enjoyment.

April

Exam success – it's never too late

Even if you are feeling the strain – don't panic there is still time to brush up on your knowledge and exam technique.

May

One month to go

Like an athlete training for an important event, you should now be reaching your peak. During the weeks before the exams:

- get plenty of rest and sleep
- refresh your memory on the difficult or essential points
- catch up if you are behind – but don't overdo it.

June

Start of GCSEs

Stay calm and don't get stressed out the night before the first exam:

- check your exam timetable and know which room the exam is in and what time it starts
- make sure you have all your equipment
- make sure you know the centre number & your candidate number

July

Congratulations your exams are over!

Good luck!

February	March	April	May	June
0	1	1	1	1
1	2	2	2	2
2	3	3	3	3
3	4	4	4	4
4	5	5	5	5
5	6	6	6	6
6	7	7	7	7
7	8	8	8	8
8	9	9	9	9
9	10	10	10	10
20	11	11	11	11
21	12	12	12	12
22	13	13	13	13
23	14	14	14	14
24	15	15	15	15
25	16	16	16	16
26	17	17	17	17
27	18	18	18	18
28	19	19	19	19
29	20	20	20	20
	21	21	21	21
	22	22	22	22
	23	23	23	23
	24	24	24	24
	25	25	25	25
	26	26	26	26
	27	27	27	27
	28	28	28	28
	29	29	29	29
	30	30	30	30
	31		31	

See overleaf for how to order...

Success with Letts

Please Photocopy this form

GCSE Revision Order Form

These books should be ordered directly from the publisher. Private orders to home addresses should include £1.00 postage & packing per book (up to £3.00 i.e. 3 books or more). There are three easy ways to place your order:

1 Telephone us on our FREEPHONE number 0800 216592
2 Fax your order to us on 0208 740 2280
3 Or send your order to our FREEPOST address:
Letts Educational, FREEPOST, London W12 8BR

Your books should arrive between 5 and 7 working days.

Order any GCSE in a Week and Passcards and save £2

Title	ISBN	Price	Qty	Value
GCSE Revision & Exam Preparation	**1 84085**			
Science Foundation Revision Notes (NEAB)	2887	£3.00		
Science Higher Revision Notes (NEAB)	2879	£3.00		
Biology Revision Notes (gen)	2909	£3.00		
Chemistry Revision Notes (gen)	2895	£3.00		
Physics Revision Notes (gen)	2917	£3.00		
Science Foundation Revision Notes (gen)	2860	£3.00		
Science Higher Revision Notes (gen)	2852	£3.00		
Maths Foundation Revision Notes (gen)	2925	£3.00		
Maths Intermediate Revision Notes (gen)	2933	£3.00		
Maths Higher Revision Notes (gen)	2941	£3.00		
Maths Foundation Revision Notes (Edexcel/London)	295X	£3.00		
Maths Intermediate Revision Notes (Edexcel/London)	2968	£3.00		
Maths Higher Revision Notes (Edexcel/London)	2976	£3.00		
GCSE French Revision Notes (includes audio CD)	2992	£4.00		
GCSE Geography Revision Notes	2984	£3.00		
GCSE Revision Skills Booklet	1449	£1.00		
Improve your GCSE Grades	2143	£1.00		
Letts Revise Guides	**1 85805**			
Biology	4206	£9.99		
Business Studies	4214	£9.99		
Chemistry	4222	£9.99		
Design and Technology	4230	£9.99		
English	4249	£9.99		
English Literature	4257	£9.99		
French (with audio CD)	4265	£13.99		
French (book only)	4273	£9.99		
Geography	4281	£9.99		
German (with audio CD)	429X	£13.99		
German (book only)	4303	£9.99		
History (1750 – present)	4311	£9.99		
Human Biology	432X	£9.99		
Information Technology	4338	£9.99		
Mathematics	4346	£9.99		
Media Studies	4354	£9.99		
Physics	4362	£9.99		
Physical Education	4370	£9.99		
Psychology	4389	£9.99		
Religious Studies	4397	£9.99		
Science	4400	£11.99		
Sociology	4419	£9.99		
Spanish (with audio CD)	4427	£13.99		
Spanish (book only)	4435	£9.99		
World History (1870 – present)	4443	£9.99		

Save £5 when you purchase Revise GCSE and a GCSE Q&A

Sub-total
Bulk purchase discount
postage
Grand Total £

Order any Revise GCSE and Questions and Answers and save £5

Title	ISBN	Price	Qty	Value
GCSE Questions and Answers	**185758**			
Biology	9505	£5.99		
Business Studies	9513	£5.99		
Chemistry	9521	£5.99		
English	953X	£5.99		
French (with audio CD)	9548	£8.99		
Geography	9556	£5.99		
German (with audio CD)	9564	£8.99		
Information Technology	9572	£5.99		
Mathematics	9580	£5.99		
Mathematics to A*	9599	£5.99		
Modern World History	9602	£5.99		
Physics	9610	£5.99		
Schools History Project	9629	£5.99		
Science	9637	£7.99		
Spanish (with audio CD)	9645	£8.99		
Revise GCSE in a Week	**1 85758**			
Biology	6956	£4.99		
Business Studies	9459	£4.99		
Chemistry	6964	£4.99		
English	6972	£4.99		
French (with audio CD)	6980	£4.99		
Geography	6999	£4.99		
Maths	7006	£4.99		
Maths to A*	9475	£4.99		
Modern World History	9467	£4.99		
Physics	7014	£4.99		
Science	7022	£4.99		
Letts Essentials for GCSE	**1 84085**			
GCSE Maths Coursework Student's Guide	1651	£1.00		
GCSE Maths for Scientists	1503	£1.00		
GCSE Maths Dictionary	1236	£1.00		
GCSE Science Foundation Coursework Student's Guide	121X	£1.00		
GCSE Science Higher Coursework Student's Guide	1457	£1.00		
GCSE Science Dictionary	1465	£1.00		
GCSE English Spelling & Vocabulary	1392	£2.00		
GCSE English Punctuation & Grammar	1406	£2.00		
GCSE French Vocabulary Book	1414	£2.00		
GCSE French Grammar Guide	0825	£2.00		
GCSE German Vocabulary Book	1422	£2.00		
GCSE Spanish Vocabulary Book	1430	£2.00		
A Level Revision & Exam Preparation	**1 XXXX**			
A Level Revision Skills Booklet	0809	£1.00		
A Level Maths Revision Notes	0922	£5.00		
A Level Chemistry Revision Notes	0949	£5.00		
A Level Biology Revision Notes	0965	£5.00		
A Level Physics Revision Notes	0981	£5.00		
A Level Business Studies Revision Notes	1007	£5.00		
A Level Psychology Revision Notes	1023	£5.00		
A Level sociology Revision Notes	1066	£5.00		
A Level computing Revision Notes	1082	£5.00		

Save £2 when you purchase one of each series

Sub-total
Bulk purchase discount
postage
Grand Total £

"special offers only available when books are purchased direct from the publisher"

☐ I enclose a cheque made payable to The Book Service Ltd

for £ ____________________

☐ Please invoice our school

☐ Please charge my MasterCard/Visa/Amex/Switch/Delta

Card number ☐☐☐☐ ☐☐☐☐ ☐☐☐☐ ☐☐☐☐

Issue number (for Switch/Delta) ☐☐ Expiry Date ☐☐

Signature ____________________

Name ____________________ Position ____________________

School ____________________

Address ____________________

Postcode ____________________

Telephone ____________________

Fax ____________________

E-mail ____________________

Every effort was made to ensure that all prices and special offers were correct at the time of going to press. However, Letts reserves the right to change these without prior notice.

Letts EDUCATIONAL

9-15 Aldine Street
London W12 8AW
Tel: 0800 216592 Fax: 0208 740 2280
E-mail: schools@lettsed.co.uk

Shape, space and measures

Properties of shape

Symmetry

Examiner's tips and your notes

Reflective symmetry

This is when both sides of the shape are the same when the **mirror line** is drawn across it. The mirror line is known as the **line of symmetry** or **axis of symmetry**.

Examples

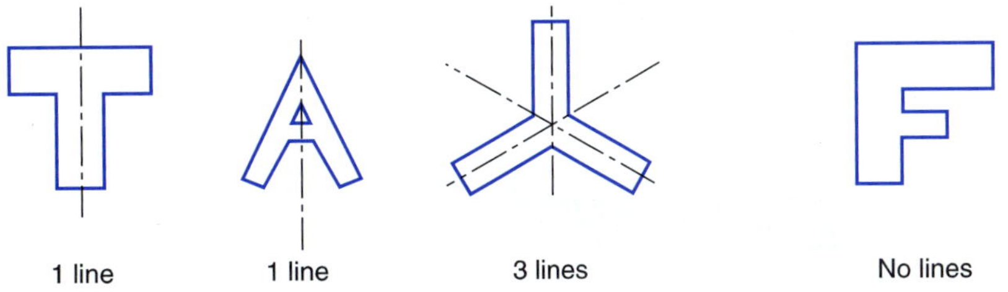

Example

Use tracing paper if it helps you.

Half a reflected shape is shown here.
The dashed line is the line of symmetry.
Copy and complete the shape.

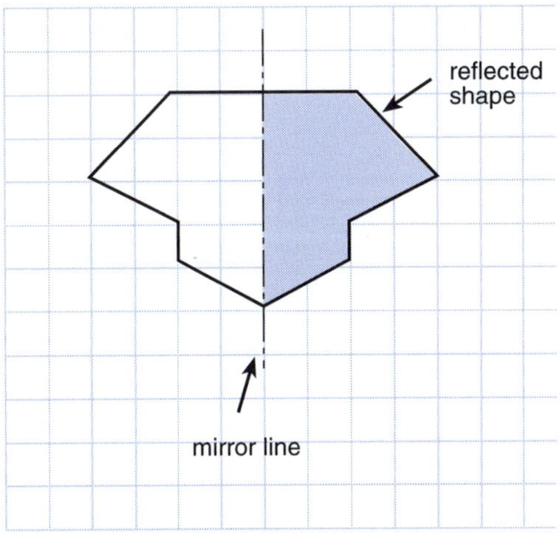

Rotational symmetry

A 2D (two-dimensional) shape has rotational symmetry if, when it is turned, it looks exactly the same. The **order** of rotational symmetry is the number of times the shape turns and looks the same.

Examples

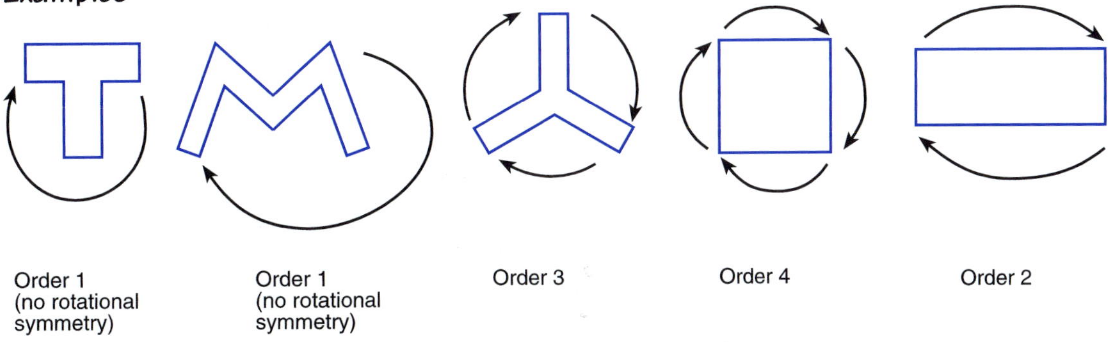

For the M shape, the shape has 1 position. It is said to have **rotational symmetry of order 1**, or **no rotational symmetry**.

Plane symmetry

This is symmetry with 3D (three-dimensional) solids only. A 3D shape has a **plane of symmetry** if the plane divides the shape into two halves and one half looks **exactly** the same as the other.

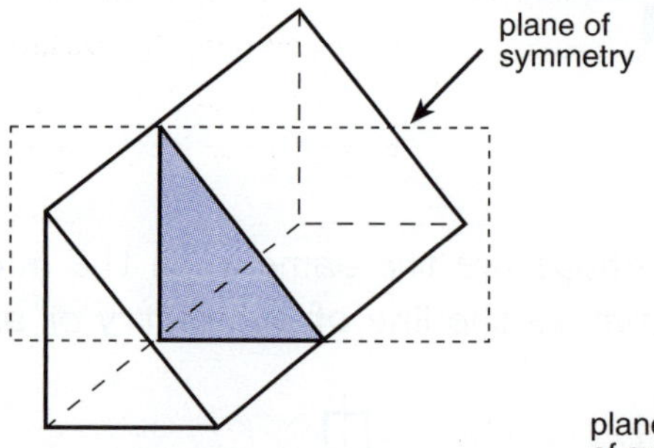

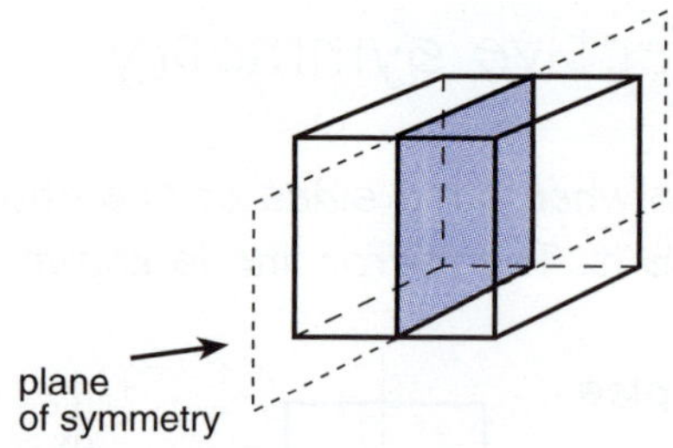

2D shapes

Triangles

There are several types of triangle.

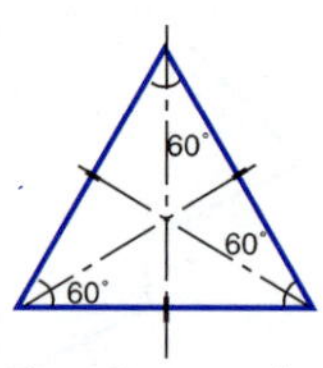

Equilateral
3 sides equal
3 angles equal

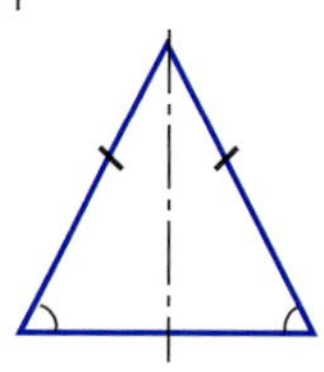

Isosceles
2 sides equal
base angles equal

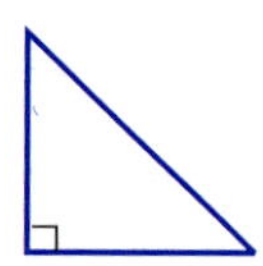

Right-angled
has a 90° angle

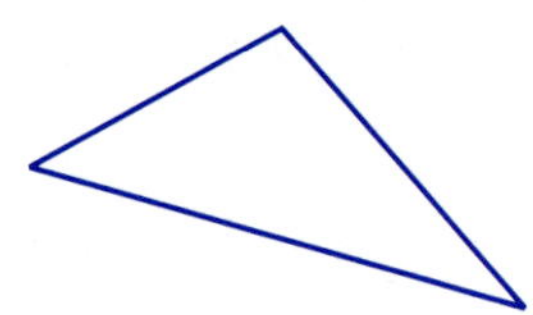

Scalene
no sides or
angles the same

Quadrilaterals

These are four-sided shapes.

You must learn the names of these shapes and their symmetrical properties.

Square

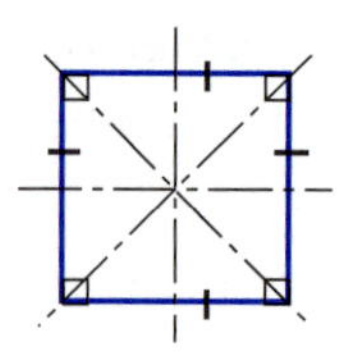

- all angles are 90°
- all sides equal
- opposite sides parallel
- 4 lines of symmetry
- rotational symmetry of order 4

Rectangle

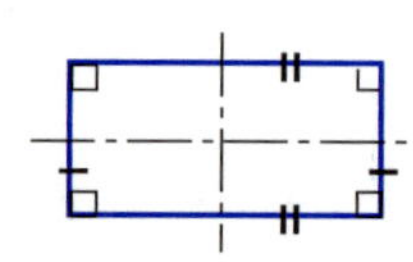

- all angles are 90°
- opposite sides equal and parallel
- 2 lines of symmetry
- rotational symmetry of order 2

Parallel lines are lines which remain the same distance apart, so they will never meet. Arrows usually indicate parallel lines.

Parallelogram

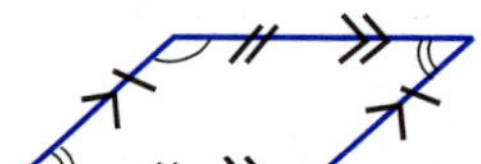

- 2 pairs of parallel sides
- opposite sides equal
- opposite angles equal
- no lines of symmetry
- rotational symmetry of order 2

Rhombus

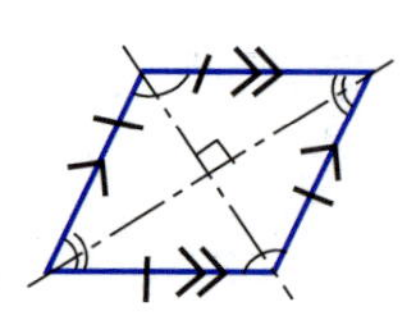

- 2 pairs of parallel sides
- all sides equal
- 2 lines of symmetry
- rotational symmetry of order 2

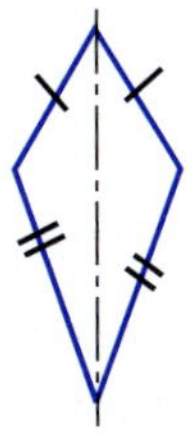

Kite

- two pairs of adjacent sides are equal
- 1 line of symmetry
- no rotational symmetry

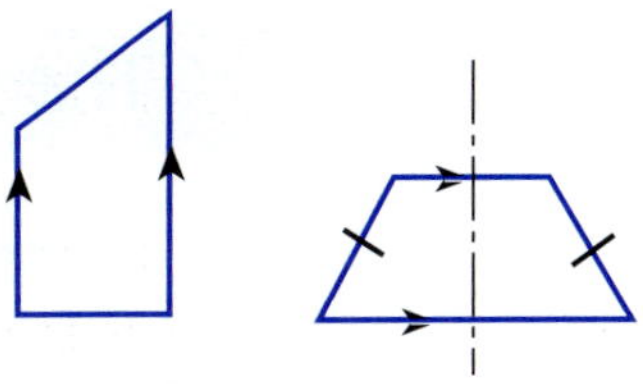

Trapezium

- one pair of parallel sides
- isosceles trapezium has 1 line of symmetry
- no rotational symmetry

Polygons

These are 2D shapes with **straight** sides.

Regular polygons are 2D shapes with all **sides** and **angles equal**.

Number of sides	Polygon
3	Triangle
4	Quadrilateral
5	Pentagon
6	Hexagon
7	Heptagon
8	Octagon

Regular pentagon

- 5 equal sides
- rotational symmetry of order 5
- 5 lines of symmetry

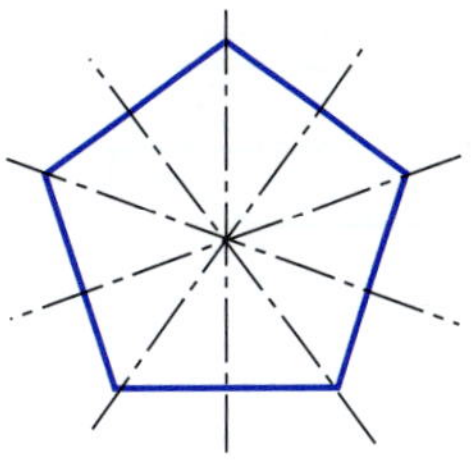

Regular hexagon

- 6 equal sides
- rotational symmetry of order 6
- 6 lines of symmetry

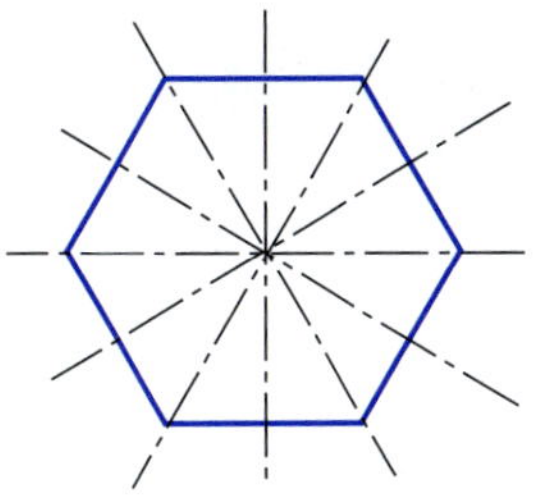

Regular octagon

- 8 equal sides
- rotational symmetry of order 8
- 8 lines of symmetry

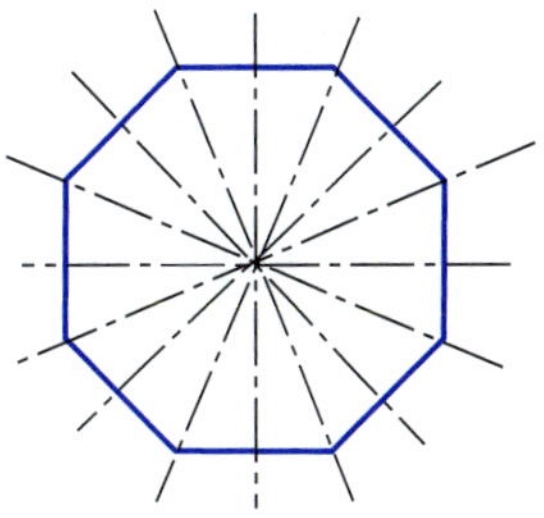

The circle

Diameter = 2 × radius

The **circumference** is the distance around the outside edge.

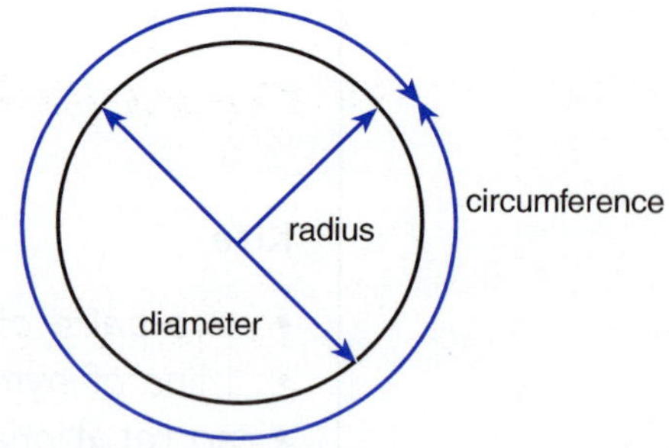

A **chord** is a line that joins two points on the circumference. The line does not go through the centre.

A **tangent** touches the circle at one point only.

An **arc** is part of the circumference.

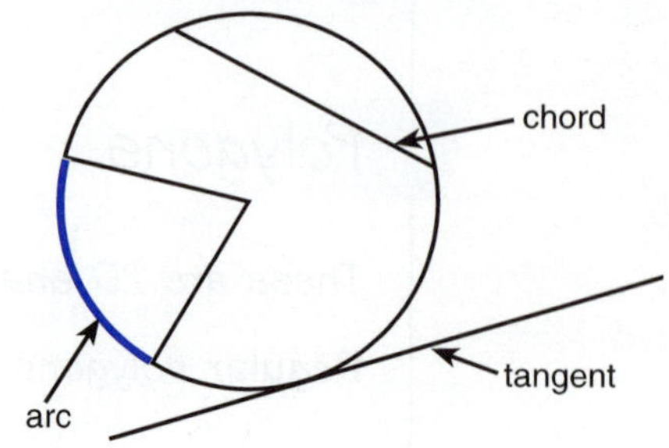

Congruent shapes

You may need to turn the paper round to spot if shapes are congruent.

These are 2D shapes which are exactly the same **size** and **shape**.

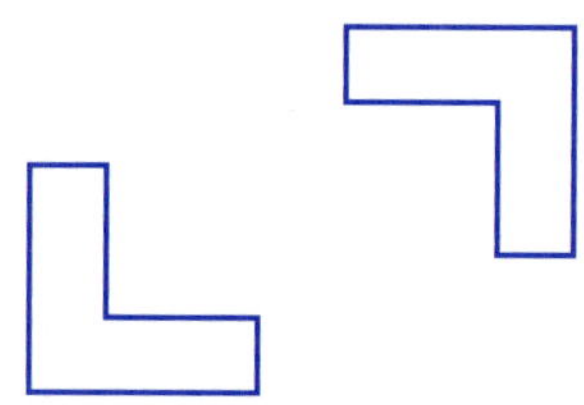

3D shapes

Remember to learn the mathematical names of these shapes.

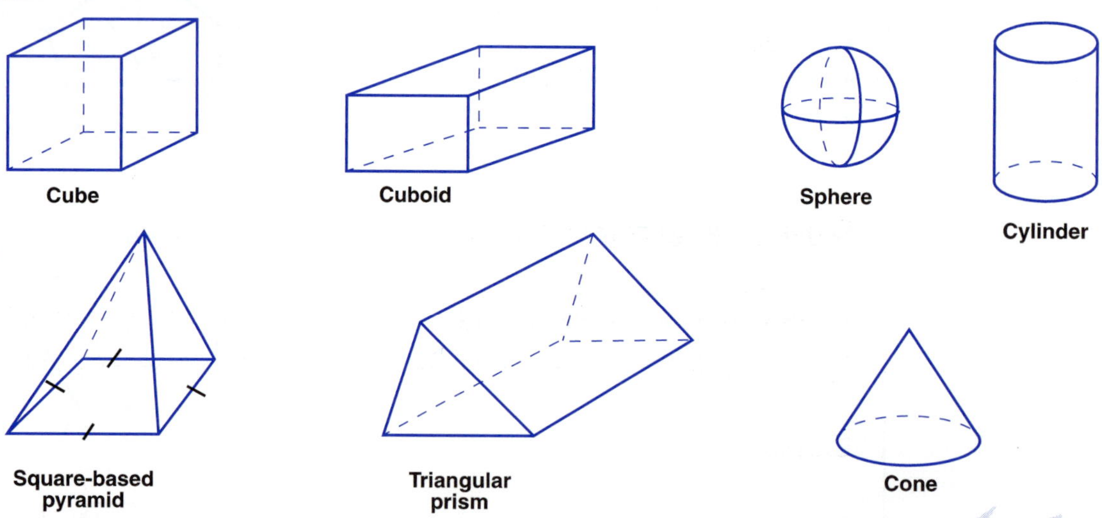

A **prism** is a solid which can be cut into slices that are all the same shape.

Faces, edges and vertices

Edges which cannot be seen are usually shown with a dotted line.

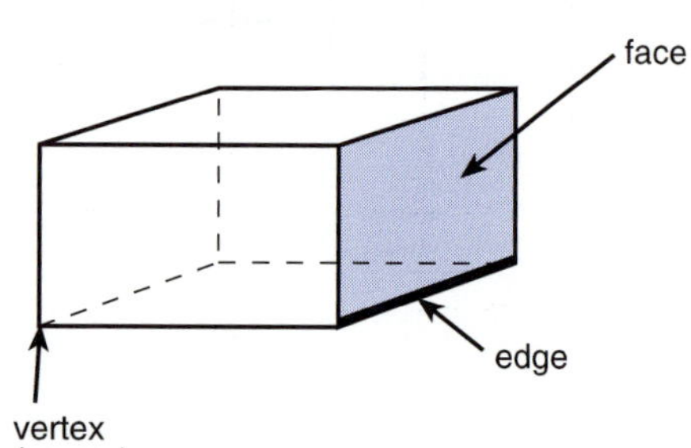

A **face** is a flat surface of a solid.

An **edge** is where two faces meet.

Vertex is another word for a corner. The plural is **vertices**.

The cuboid has 6 faces, 8 vertices and 12 edges.

Drawing shapes

Nets of solids

When asked to draw a net, make sure you measure the sides accurately.

The net of a 3D shape is the 2D shape which is folded to make the 3D shape.

Examples

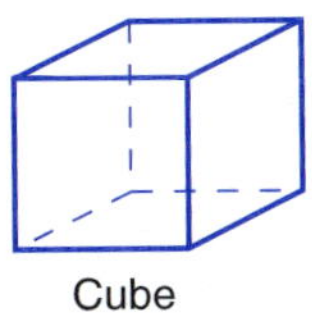

Cube

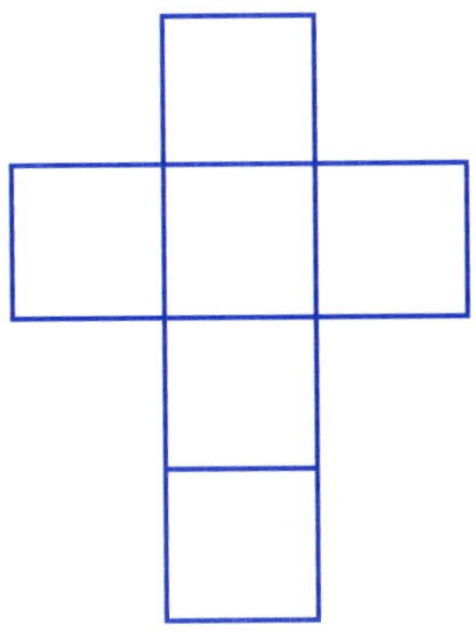

Net of cube

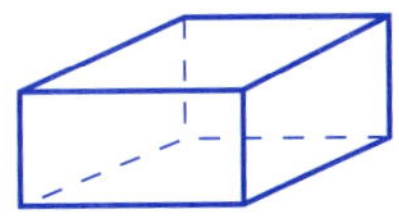

Cuboid

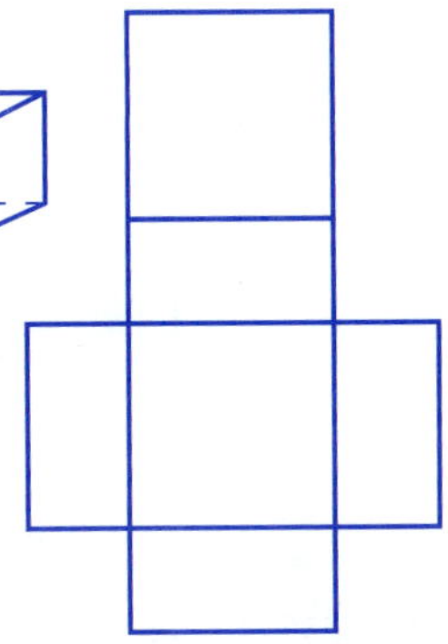

Net of cuboid

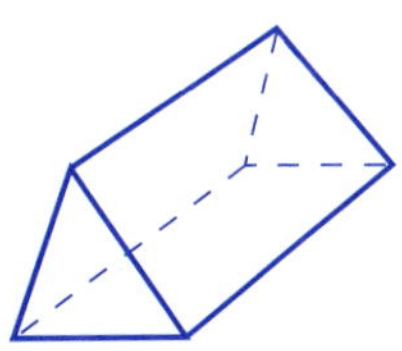

Triangular prism

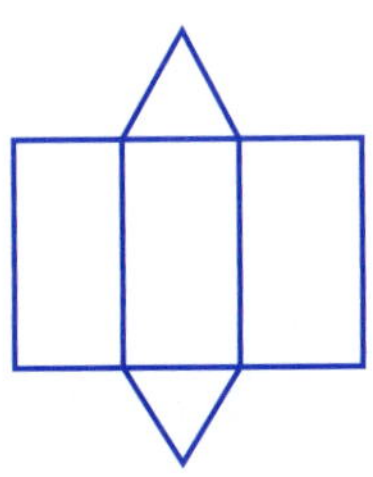

Net of prism

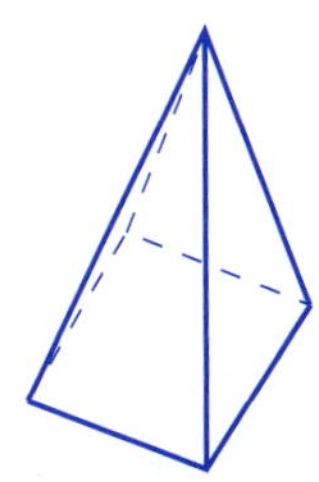

Square-based pyramid

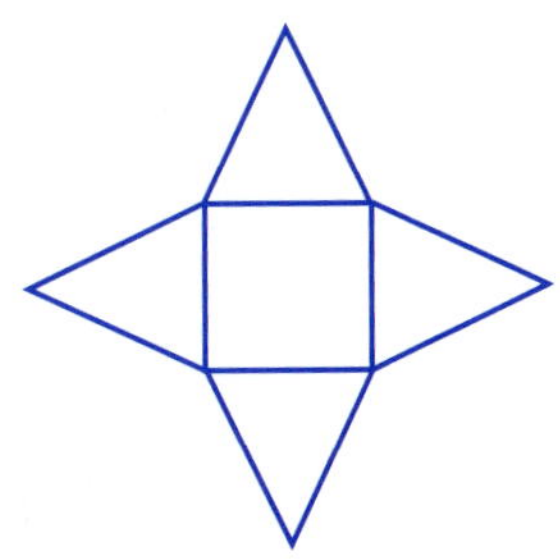

Net of pyramid

Plans and elevations

A **plan** is what is seen if a 3D shape is looked down on **from above**.

An **elevation** is seen if the 3D shape is looked at from the **side** or **front**.

Example

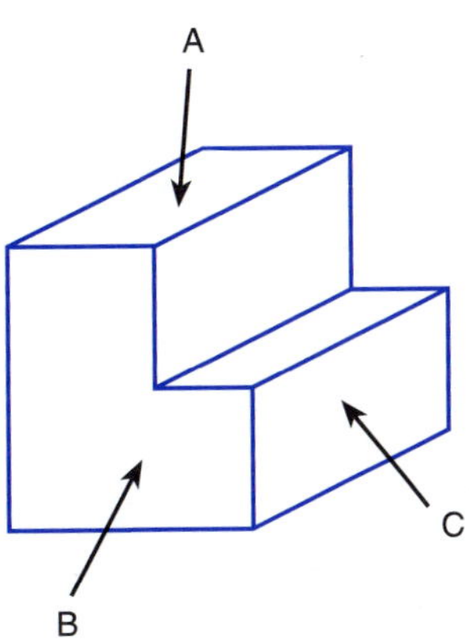

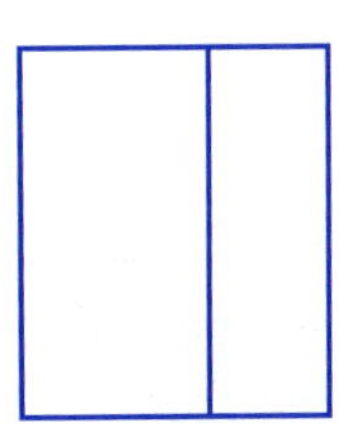

Plan (from A)

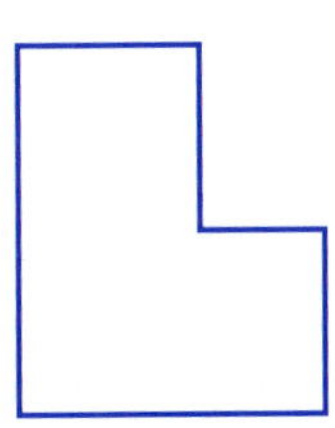

Front elevation (from B)

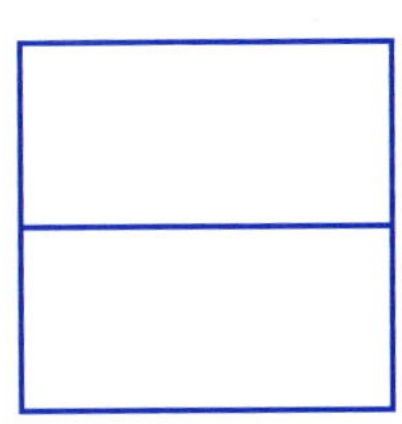

Side elevation (from C)

Angles

An angle is an amount of **turning** or **rotation**. Angles are measured using a protractor, in degrees.

A circle is divided into 360 parts. Each part is called a **degree** and is represented by a small circle °.

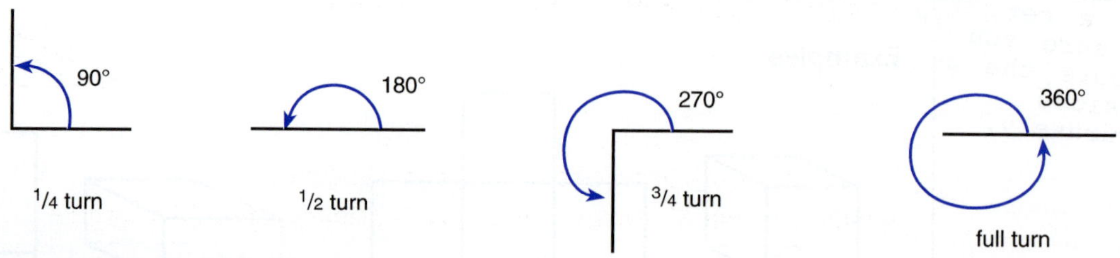

Names of angles

A 90° angle is usually shown with a square.

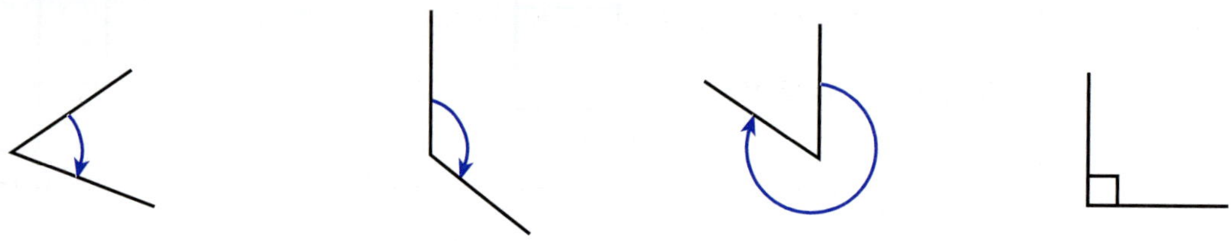

An **acute** angle is between 0° and 90°.

An **obtuse** angle is between 90° and 180°.

A **reflex** angle is greater than 180°.

A **right** angle is 90°.

Measuring angles using a protractor

A protractor is used to measure the size of an angle.

When measuring angles, count the degree lines carefully and always double check!

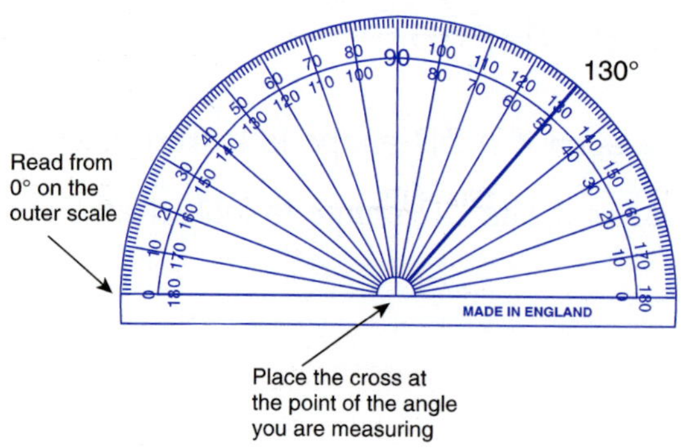

Beware! Make sure you put the 0° line at the start position and read from the correct scale.

For the above angle, measure on the outer scale since you must start from 0°.

Angle facts

Angles on a **straight line** add up to **180°**.

$a + b + c = 180°$

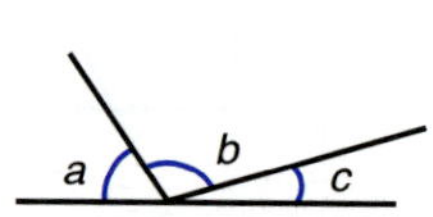

Angles that meet at a **point** add up to **360°**.

$a + b + c + d = 360°$

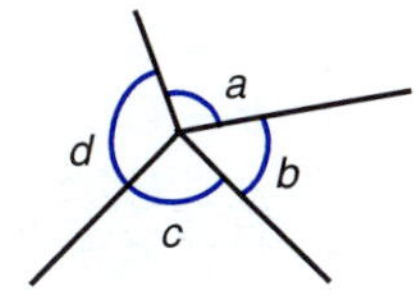

Angles in a **triangle** add up to **180°**.

$a + b + c = 180°$

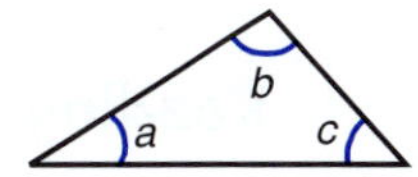

Angles in a **quadrilateral** add up to **360°**.

$a + b + c + d = 360°$

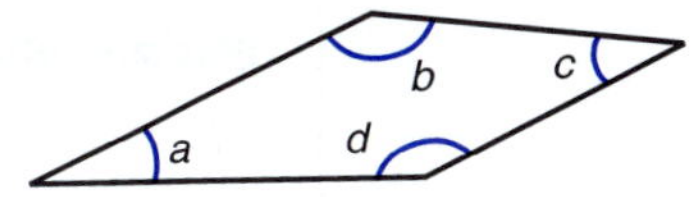

Where two straight lines cross, the **opposite** angles are **equal**. These are called **vertically opposite angles**.

$a = b$ and $c = d$

Also $a + d$ and $b + c$ each add up to 180° because they are on a straight line.

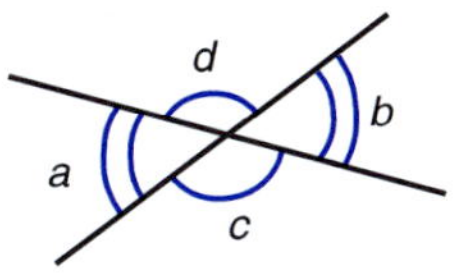

Angles in parallel lines

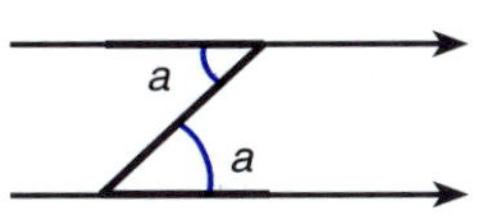

Alternate (Z) angles are **equal**.

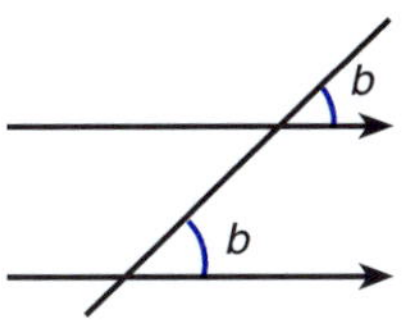

Corresponding angles are **equal**.

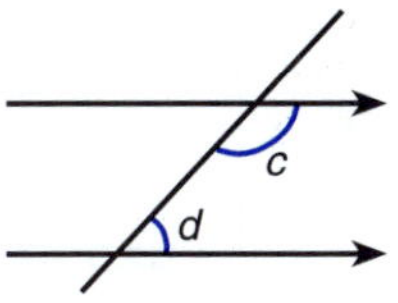

Supplementary angles add up to **180°**.
$c + d = 180°$

Examples (Not to scale)

Find the size of the missing angles.

$a + 135° = 180°$
$a = 180° - 135°$
$= 45°$

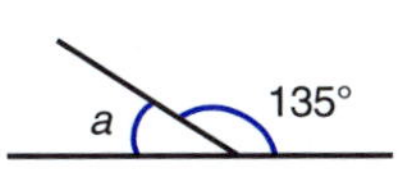

$p + 90° + 120° = 360°$
$p + 210° = 360°$
$p = 360° - 210°$
$= 150°$

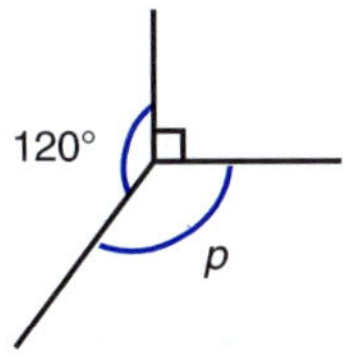

Make sure you show all of your working out.

$a + a + 80° = 180°$
$2a + 80° = 180°$
$2a = 180° - 80°$
$2a = 100°$
$a = \frac{100°}{2} = 50°$

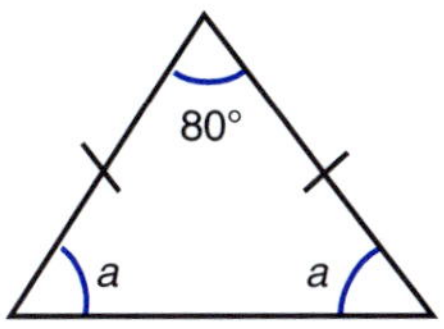

Remember for an isosceles triangle the base angles are equal.

$x + 70° + 30° = 180°$
$x + 100° = 180°$
$x = 180° - 100°$
$= 80°$

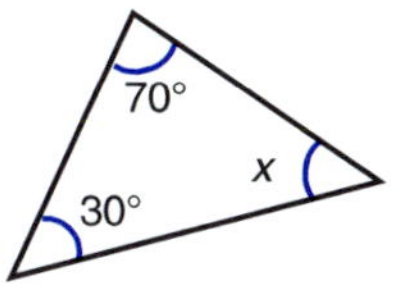

$x + 110° + 30° + 70° = 360°$
$x + 210° = 360°$
$x = 360° - 210°$
$= 150°$

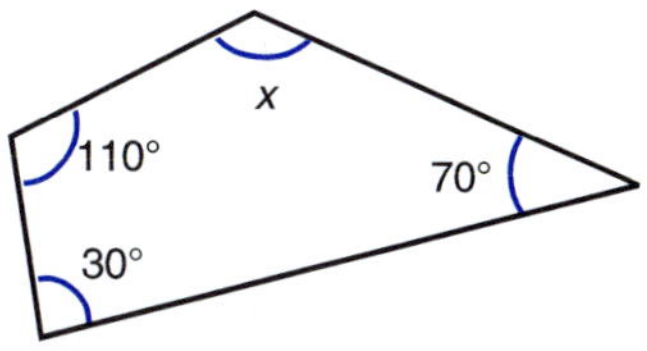

$y = 50°$ (opposite)
$x = 130°$ ($50° + 130° = 180°$)
$z = 130°$ (opposite)

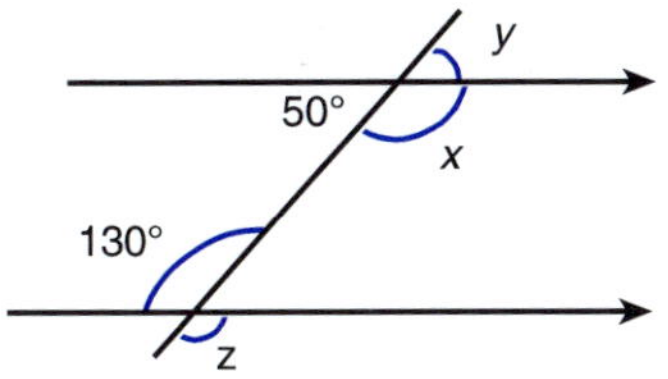

$a = 120°$ (angles on a straight line)
$b = 60°$ (vertically opposite)
$c = 60°$ (corresponding to b)
$d = 60°$ (vertically opposite to c)

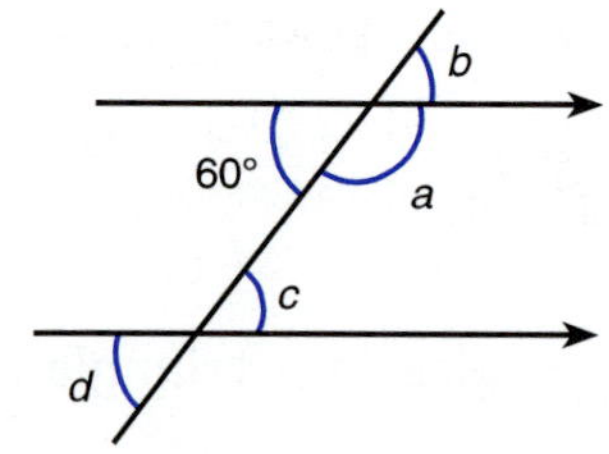

Reading angles

When asked to find angle XYZ or <XYZ or $X\hat{Y}Z$, find the **middle lettered** angle, angle Y.

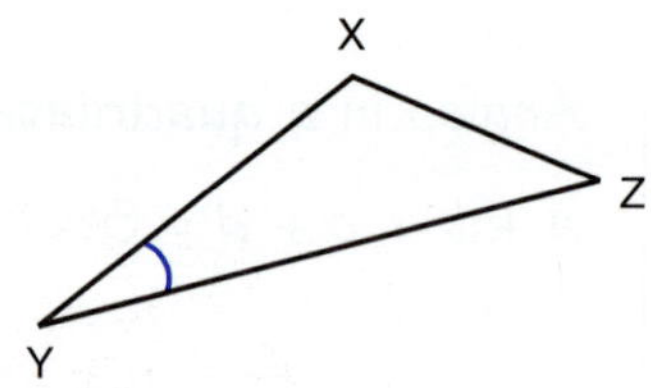

Angles in polygons

There are two types of angle: **interior** (inside), **exterior** (outside).

For a regular polygon with n sides:

- sum of the exterior angles = 360°, so exterior angle = $360° \div n$
- interior angle + exterior angle = 180°
- sum of the interior angles = $(n - 2) \times 180°$

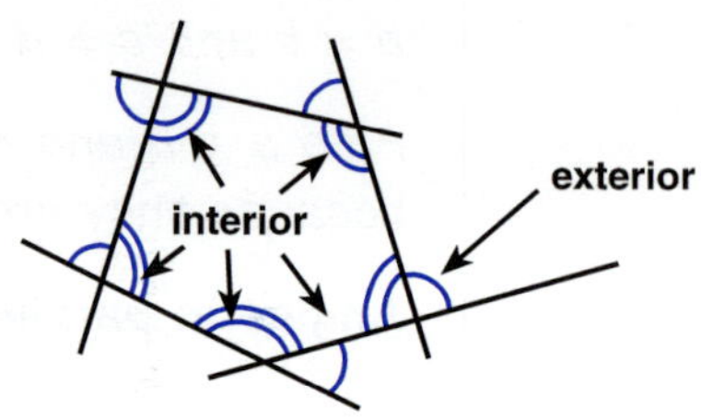

Example

Calculate the size of an interior and exterior angle of a regular hexagon.

A hexagon has 6 sides, so $n = 6$.

Exterior angle = $\frac{360°}{6} = 60°$ (exterior angle = $360° \div n$)
Interior angle = $180° - 60° = 120°$ (interior + exterior = 180°)

Example

Find the sum of the interior angles of a regular pentagon.

A pentagon has 5 sides.

Sum of interior angles $= (n - 2) \times 180°$
$= (5 - 2) \times 180°$
$= 3 \times 180° = 540°$

Questions

1 What are the names of the three types of symmetry?

2 The dashed lines are the lines of symmetry. Complete the shape so that it is symmetrical.

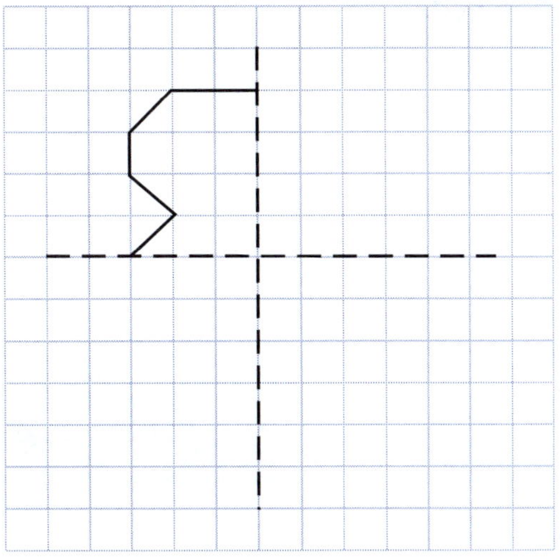

3 Sketch and name the different types of quadrilaterals. (There are 6.)

4 What is the name of an eight-sided polygon?

5 Draw a sketch of the net of a square-based pyramid.

6 Draw a sketch of the plan and elevations from A and B of this solid.

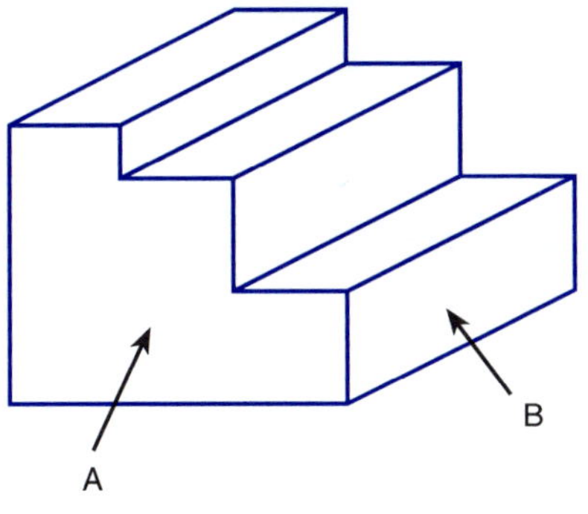

7 Calculate the size of the angles labelled with letters.

(Not to scale)

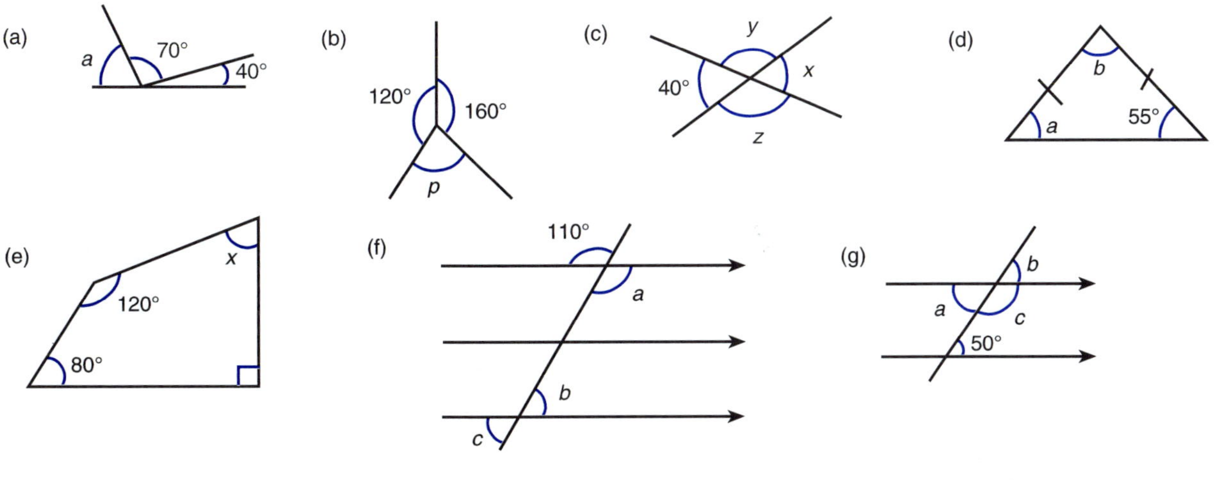

Properties of position, movement and transformation

Tessellations

Examiner's tips and your notes

A **tessellation** is a pattern of 2D shapes which fit together without leaving any gaps. For shapes to tessellate, the angles at a point must add up to 360°.

Examples

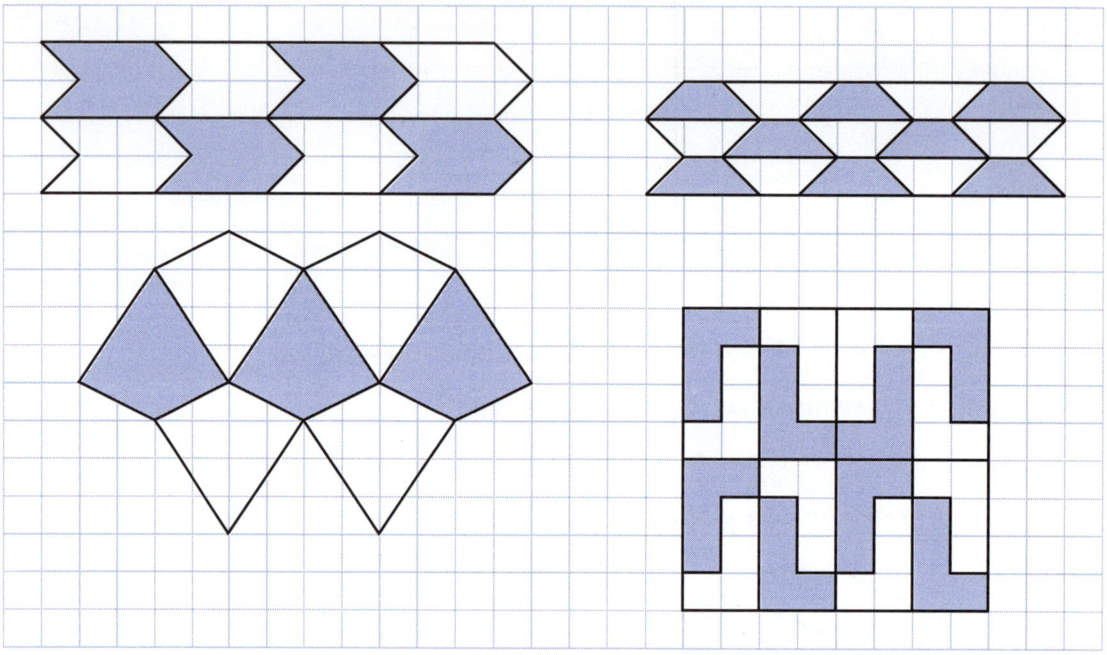

Compass directions and bearings

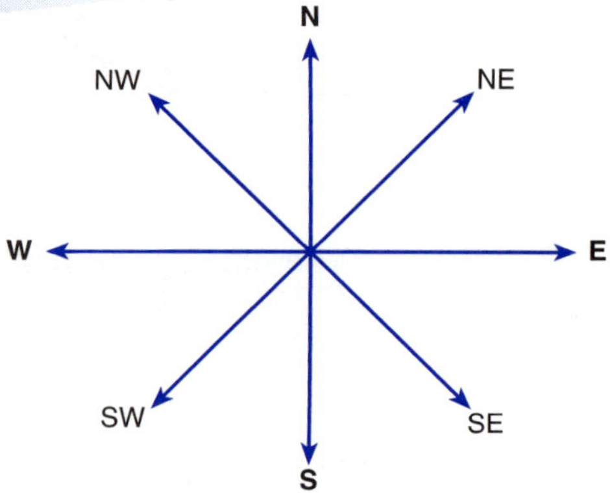

The diagram shows the points of the compass.

For other directions, for example between north-west and north, **bearings** are used.

- Bearings give a direction in degrees.
- Bearings are always measured from the **north** in a **clockwise** direction.
- They must have **3 figures**.
- The word **from** indicates the position of the north line from which the angle is measured.

Remember: clockwise is in this direction.

Examples

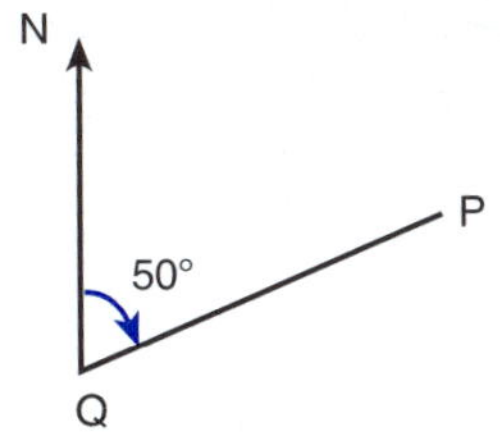

Bearing of P **from** Q
= 050°

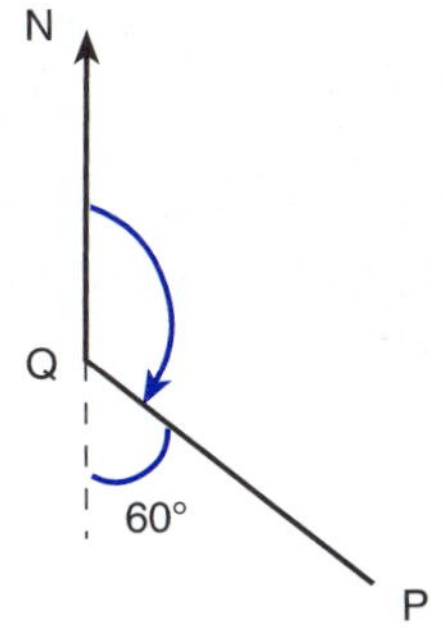

Bearing of P **from** Q
= 180° – 60° = 120°

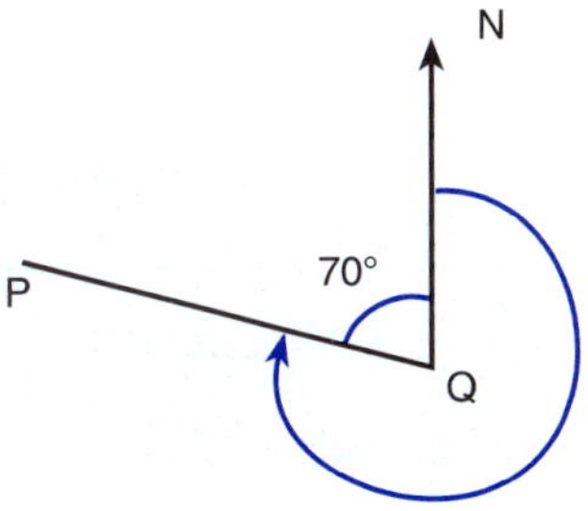

Bearing of P **from** Q
= 360° – 70° = 290°

50° is written as 050° because it has to be 3 figures.

Notice that since we are finding the bearing of P **from Q**, the north line is placed at Q and the bearing is measured in a clockwise direction from this north line.

Angle facts are used when finding bearings.

When finding a **back bearing**, that is the bearing of Q **from P** above:

- draw a north line at P;
- the two north lines are parallel lines, so the angle properties of parallel lines are used.

Examples (Not to scale)

- Put the north line at P.
- Measure in a clockwise direction from P.
- Bearing of Q **from P** is 50° + 180° = 230°.

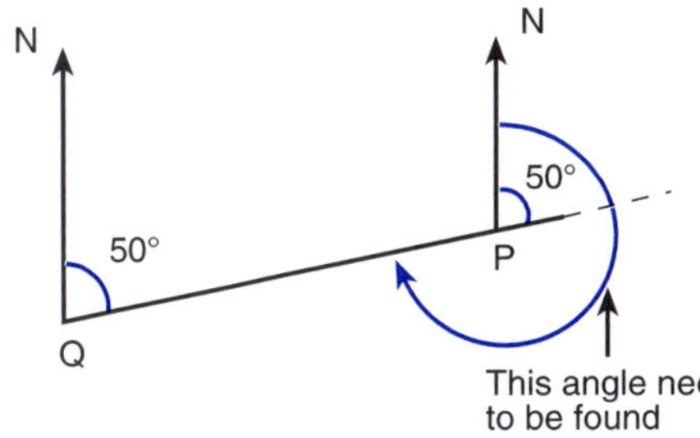

Look for alternate or corresponding angles when finding back bearings.

- Place the north line at P.
- Measure in a clockwise direction from P.
- Bearing of Q **from P** is 360° – 60° = 300°.

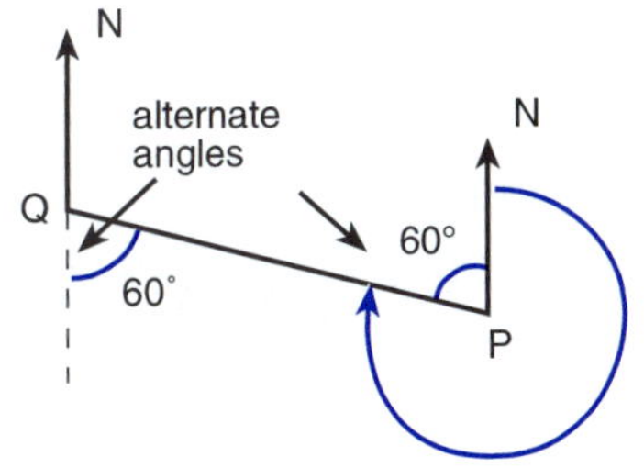

Transformations

A **transformation** changes the **position** or **size** of a shape.

There are four types of transformation: translations, reflections, rotations and enlargements.

Translations

Translations move figures from one place to another. The size or shape of the figure is not changed.

Example

Draw the image of triangle ABC after a translation of 5 squares to the right and 1 square down.

When translating, each vertex (corner) moves exactly the same amount. All the vertices are displaced 5 squares to the right and 1 square down.

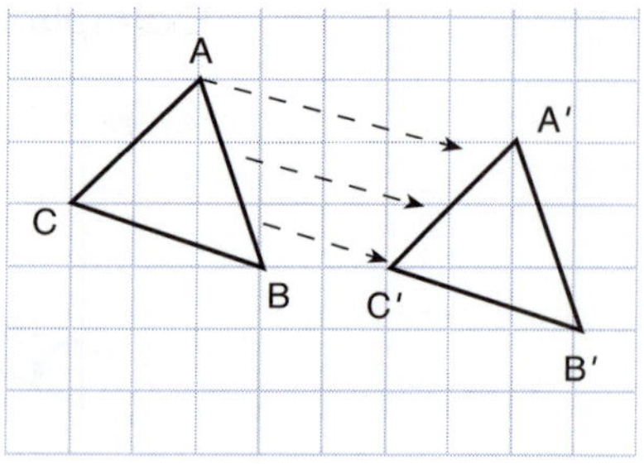

It is best to translate each vertex one at a time then join up the points.

Example

Draw the image of ABCD after a translation of 4 squares to the left and 3 squares up.

ABCD and A'B'C'D' are **congruent**.

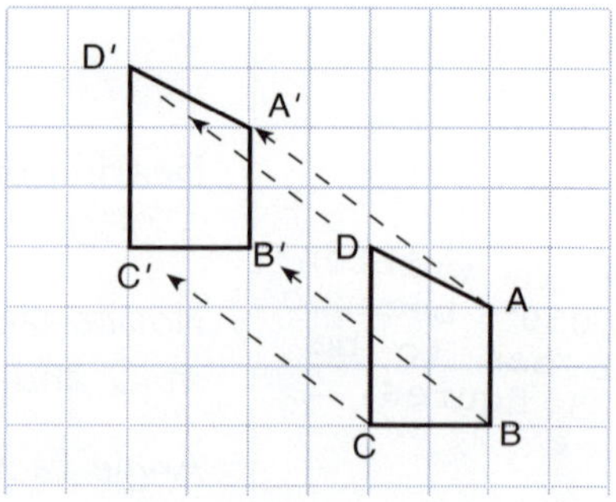

Reflections

Reflections create an image of an object on the other side of a mirror line. The mirror line is known as an **axis of reflection**. The size or shape of the figure is not changed.

Example

Reflect triangle ABC in the mirror line.

Plot the image points first. They are the same distance from the mirror as the object.

Join up the image points.

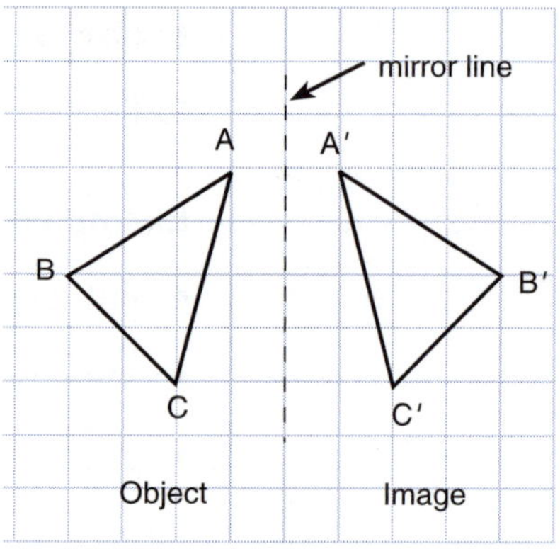

The x and y axes act as the mirror line.

Example

Reflect triangle ABC in:

(a) the x axis and call it P;

(b) the y axis and call it Q.

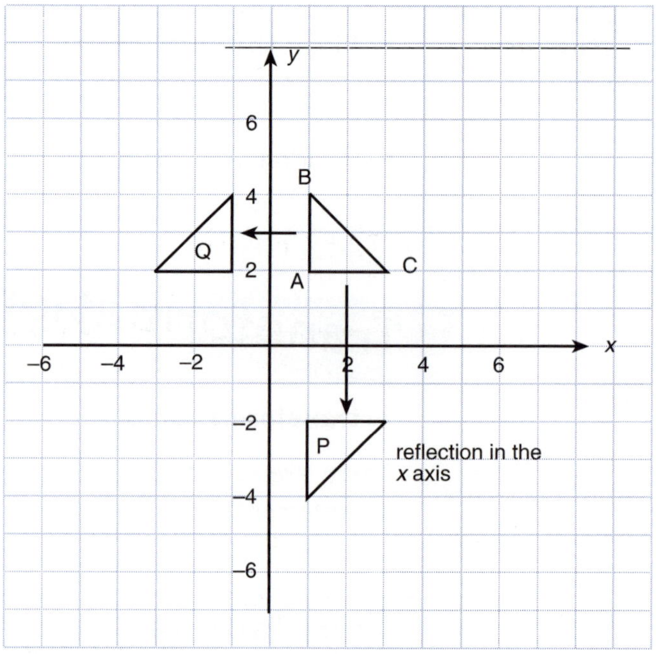

Example

Reflect triangle ABC in:

(a) the line x = 4 and call it R;

(b) the line y = −2 and call it S.

Draw in the lines x = 4 and y = −2 first; these then act as the mirror lines.

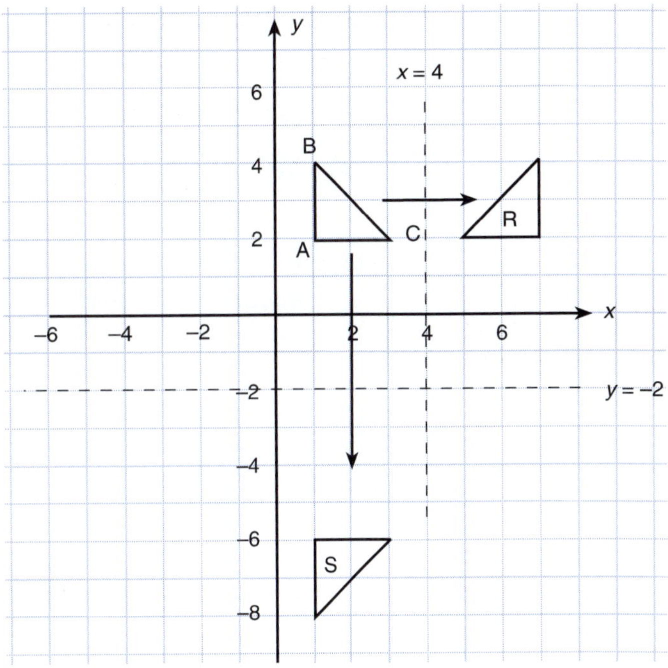

Example

Reflect triangle ABC in:

(a) the line y = x and call it T;

(b) the line y = −x and call it W.

When describing reflections, the axis of reflection (or mirror line) must be written down.

Take care when reflecting in the lines y = x and y = −x.

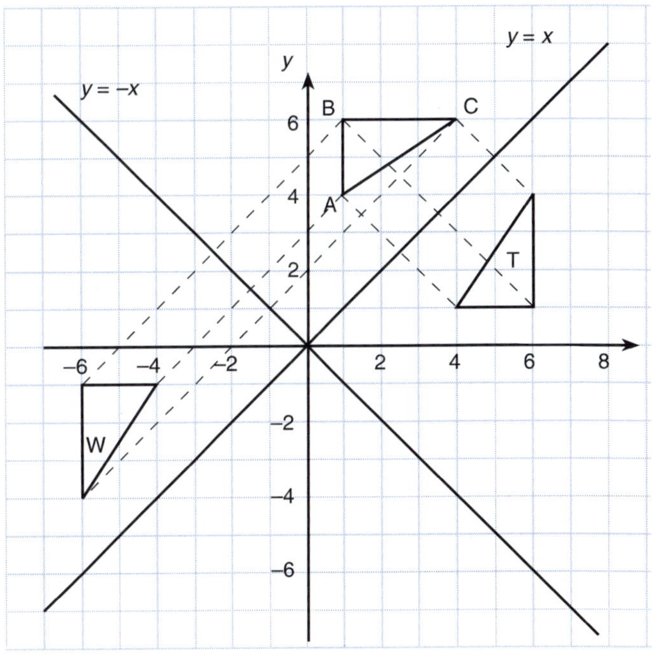

Rotations

Rotations **turn** a figure through an angle about some fixed point. This fixed point is called the **centre of rotation**.

The size or shape of the figure is not changed.

When describing a rotation give:

- the **centre** of rotation;
- the **direction** of the rotation (clockwise or anticlockwise);
- the **angle** of the rotation.

Always ask to use tracing paper in the exam as it makes rotations much easier to do.

Example

This is a 90° rotation about O, in a clockwise direction (also known as a $\frac{1}{4}$ turn clockwise).

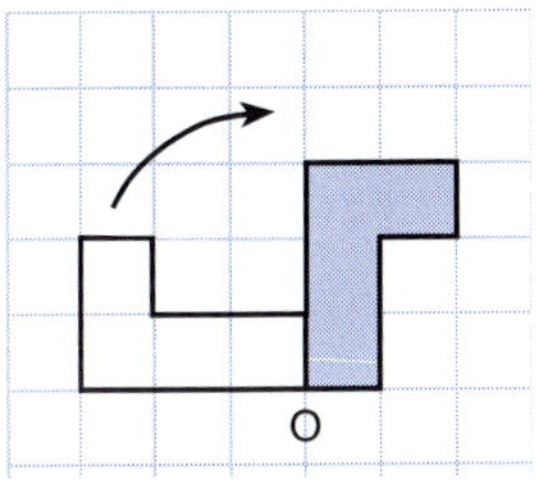

Example

Rotate triangle ABC:

(a) 90° clockwise about (0, 0) and call it P;

(b) 180° about (0, 0) and call it Q;

(c) 90° anticlockwise about (0, 0) and call it R.

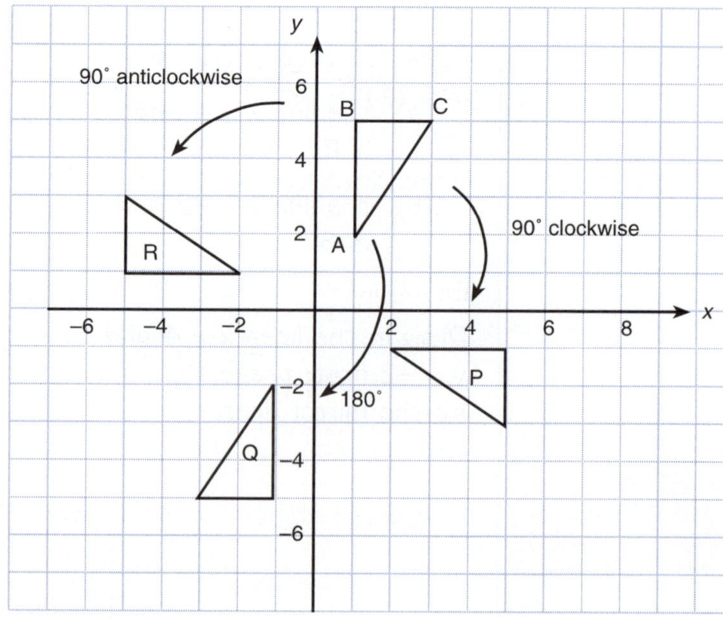

Remember that 90° is a quarter turn and 180° is half a turn.

Enlargements

These change the **size** but not the shape of an object. The **scale factor** indicates how many times the lengths of the original figure have changed size. The **centre of enlargement** is the point from which the enlargement takes place.

If the scale factor is greater than 1, the shape becomes bigger.

When describing enlargements, state the centre of enlargement and the scale factor of enlargement.

Example

Enlarge the rectangle ABCD by a scale factor of 3, centre of enlargement at A.

Notice that each side of the enlargement is three times the size of the original.

A′B′ = 3AB

A′D′ = 3AD

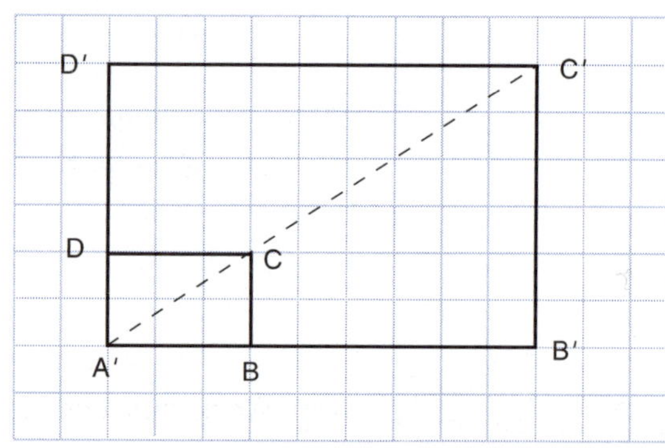

Example

Enlarge triangle ABC by a scale factor of 2, centre of enlargement the origin (0, 0). Call the enlarged shape A′B′C′.

When the centre of enlargement is the origin, to find the position of the enlarged shape just multiply the coordinates by the scale factor.

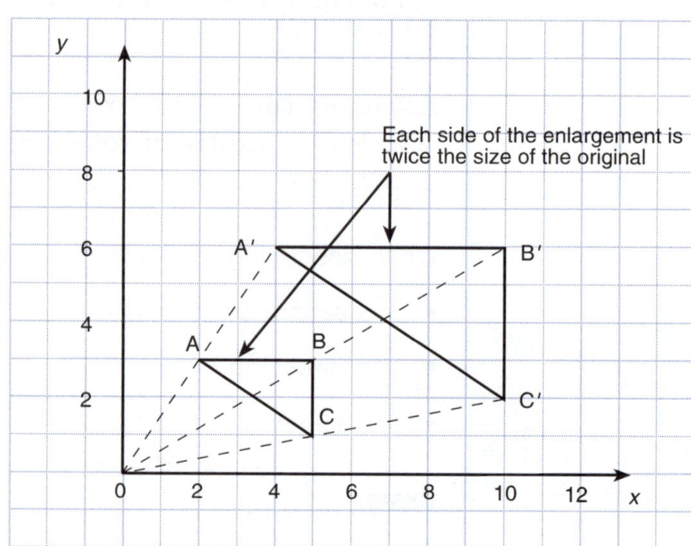

Scale drawings

Scale drawings are very useful for measuring lengths which cannot be measured directly.

Example

A ladder rests against a wall, so that the foot of the ladder is 8 metres from the wall. The ladder makes an angle of 37° with the ground. Using a scale of 1 cm to 2 m, make an accurate scale drawing. How long is the ladder and how far up the wall does the ladder reach?

A scale of 1 cm to 2 m means that 8 m is 8 ÷ 2 = 4 cm on the diagram.

Use a protractor to measure the angle and a ruler to measure the distances.

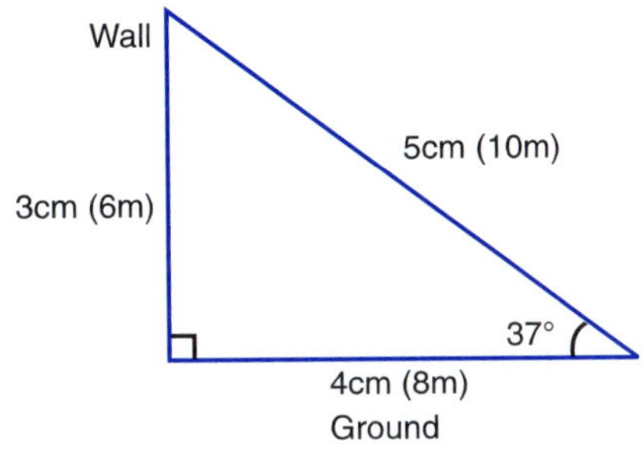

The length of the ladder in the diagram is 5 cm; so the ladder is 5 × 2 = 10 metres long.

The height up the wall in the diagram is 3 cm; this is 3 × 2 = 6 metres in real life.

Maps and diagrams

Scales are often used on maps. They are usually written as a ratio.

Example

The scale on a road map is 1 : 25 000. Bury and Oldham are 20 cm apart on the map. Work out the real distance between Bury and Oldham in km.

1 : 25 000

1 cm on the map represents 25 000 cm in real life.

20 cm represents 20 × 25 000 = 500 000 cm.

Divide by 100 to change cm to m.

500 000 ÷ 100 = 5000

Divide by 1000 to change m to km.

5000 ÷ 1000 = 5 km

A scale of 1 : 25 000 means that 1 cm on the scale drawing represents a real length of 25 000 cm.

Example

A house plan has a scale of 1 : 30. If the width of the house on the plan is 64 cm, what would this represent in real life?

Scales are often used on diagrams. For example, architects use scales when drawing plans of houses.

1 cm represents 30 cm.

64 cm represents 64 × 30 = 1920 cm

1920 ÷ 100 = 19.2 metres

In real life the width of the house would be 19.2 metres.

Properties of position, movement and transformation

Questions

1 Copy and continue the tessellation of this shape. (Include at least six more.)

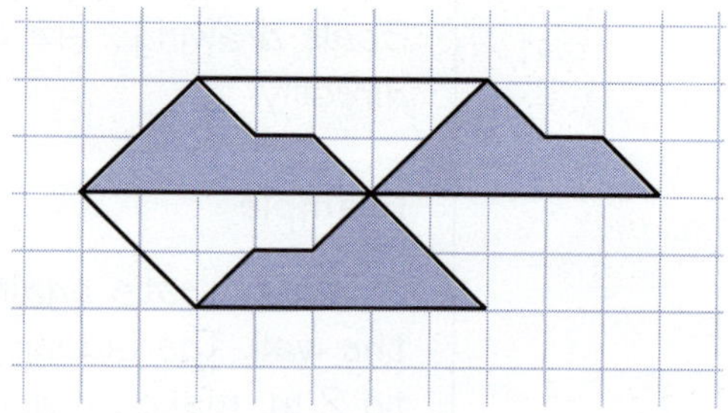

2 What are the bearings of A from B in the following diagrams?

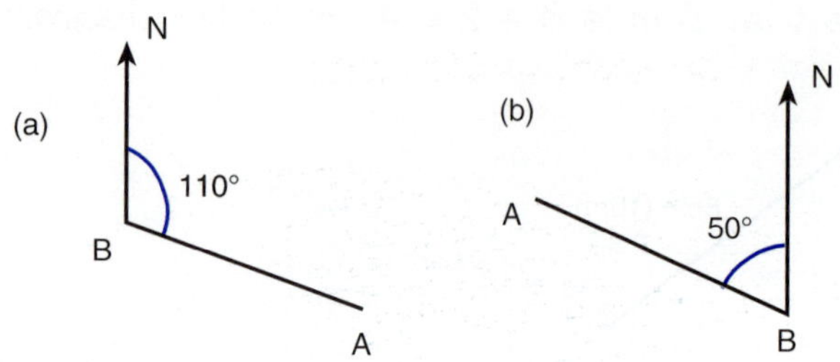

3 On the grid:

(a) Reflect triangle R in the x axis. Call it T.

(b) Rotate triangle R 90° anticlockwise about the origin. Call it P.

(c) Reflect triangle R in the line x = 3. Call it N.

(d) Rotate triangle R 180° about the origin. Call it W.

(e) Translate triangle R 3 squares to the right and 2 squares down. Call it V.

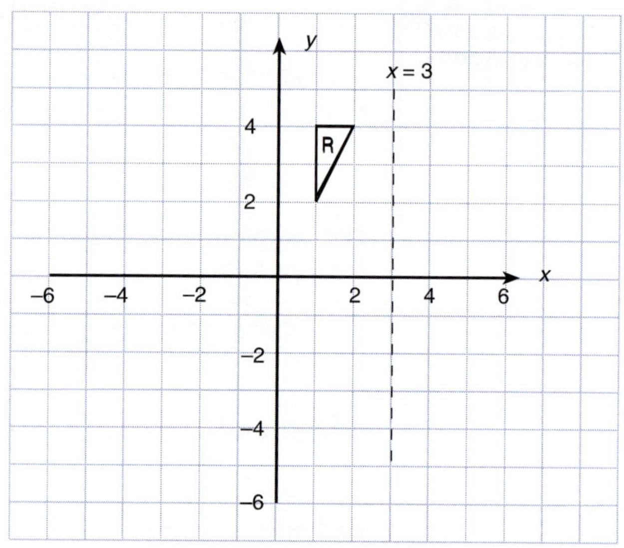

4 Enlarge shape PQRST with a scale factor 2, centre of enlargement at P.

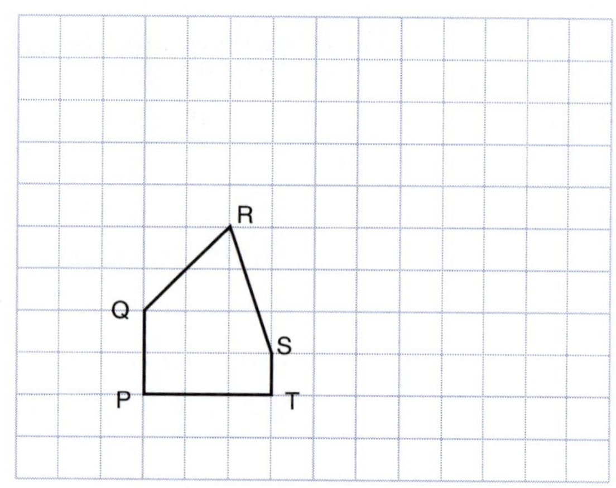

5 The scale on a road map is 1 : 50 000. If two towns are 14 cm apart on the map, work out the real distance between them.

Measures

Estimating

Examiner's tips and your notes

Estimates using metric and imperial units need to be made all the time.
- **Metric** units include kilometres (km), metres (m), kilograms (kg) etc.
- **Imperial** units include miles, yards, pounds, pints etc.

Estimating lengths

Lengths and distances can be measured using these types of units:
- **Metric**: kilometres (km), metres (m), centimetres (cm) and millimetres (mm);
- **Imperial**: feet, inches, yards and miles.

Some common estimates include:
- a door is about 2 metres high or about $6\frac{1}{2}$ feet;
- a 30 cm ruler is about 1 foot long.

Estimating capacities

Capacity is a measure of how much a container can hold.
- **Metric**: millilitres (ml), centilitres (cl), litres (l);
- **Imperial**: gallons, pints.

Some common estimates include:
- a 1 pint milk carton holds about 570 ml;
- a petrol can holds 1 gallon or 4.5 litres;
- a can of pop holds about 300 ml or $\frac{1}{2}$ pint.

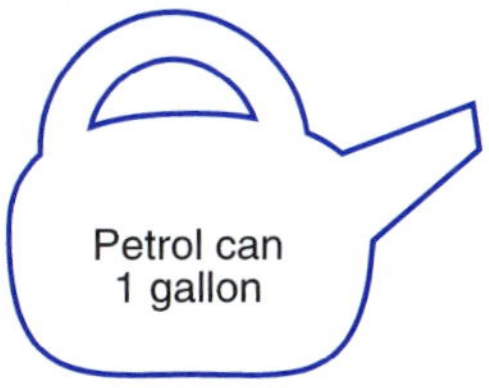

Estimating weights (masses)

Weights can be measured in these units:
- **Metric**: milligrams (mg), grams (g), kilograms (kg), tonnes (t).
- **Imperial**: ounces (oz), pounds (lb), stones, tons.

Some common estimates are:
- A 1 kg bag of sugar weighs about 2.2 pounds.
- A pound packet of butter weighs about 400 g.

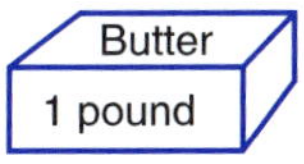

Units

Metric units

You need to learn these metric equivalents.

Length	Weight	Capacity
10 mm = 1 cm	1000 mg = 1 g	1000 ml = 1 l
100 cm = 1 m	1000 g = 1 kg	100 cl = 1 l
1000 m = 1 km	1000 kg = 1 tonne	1000 cm^3 = 1 l

Converting metric units

If changing from **small** units to **large** units (for example, g to kg), **divide**.

If changing from **large** units to **small** units (for example, km to m), **multiply**.

Examples

(a) Change 60 mm into cm.

mm are smaller than cm, so divide by the number of mm in a cm.

$60 \div 10 = 6$ cm

(b) Change 2.6 l into ml.

Check that your answers seem sensible.

l are bigger than ml, so multiply by the number of ml in a l.

$2.6 \times 1000 = 2600$ ml

(c) Change 250 g into kg.

g are smaller than kg, so divide by the number of g in a kg.

$250 \div 1000 = 0.25$ kg

(d) Change 6 km into mm.

km are bigger than mm, so multiply by the number of m in a km, cm in a m, mm in a cm.

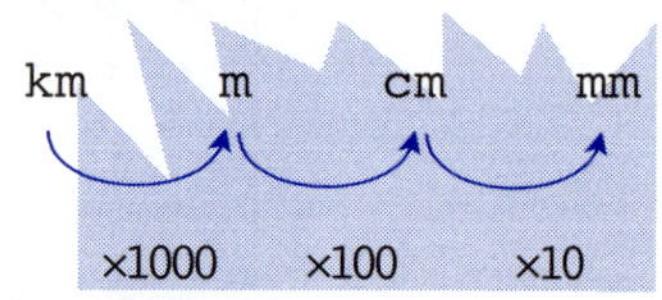

$6 \times 1000 \times 100 \times 10 = 6\ 000\ 000$ mm

Imperial units

Length	Weight	Capacity
1 foot = 12 inches	1 stone = 14 pounds (lb)	20 fluid ounces (fl oz) = 1 pint (pt)
1 yard = 3 feet	1 pound = 16 ounces (oz)	8 pints = 1 gallon

Comparisons between metric and imperial units

The conversions in **bold** type need to be learnt.

Length	Weight	Capacity
2.5 cm ≈ 1 inch	25 g ≈ 1 ounce	**1 litre ≈ $1\frac{3}{4}$ pints**
30 cm ≈ 1 foot	**1 kg ≈ 2.2 pounds**	**4.5 litres ≈ 1 gallon**
1 m ≈ 39 inches		
8 km ≈ 5 miles		

Most of the comparisons between metric and imperial units are only approximate.

Example

Change 25 km into miles.

8 km ≈ 5 miles. 1 km ≈ $\frac{5}{8}$ miles = 0.625 miles

So 25 km ≈ 25 × 0.625 miles

= 15.625 miles

Check that your answer seems sensible.

Example

A plate is 6 inches across. Roughly how many cm is this?

2.5 cm ≈ 1 inch So 6 inches ≈ 6 × 2.5 = 15 cm

Reading scales

Decimals are usually used when reading off scales. Measuring jugs, rulers, weighing scales are all examples of scales which have decimals.

Examples

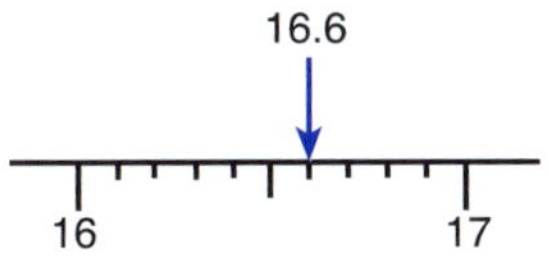

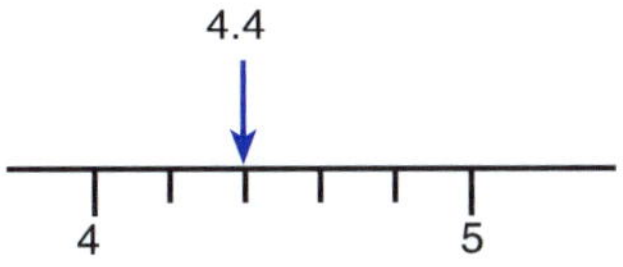

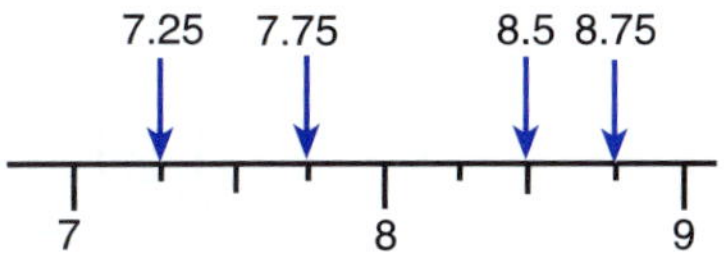

There are 10 spaces between the 16 and 17. Each space is 0.1.

There are 5 spaces between the 4 and 5. Each space is 0.2.

There are 4 spaces between the 7 and 8. Each space is 0.25.

Perimeter of 2D shapes

The **perimeter** is the distance around the outside edge of the shape.

Examples

Find the perimeter of these shapes.

(a)

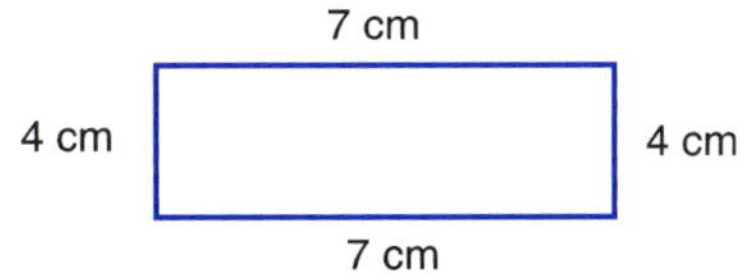

(b)

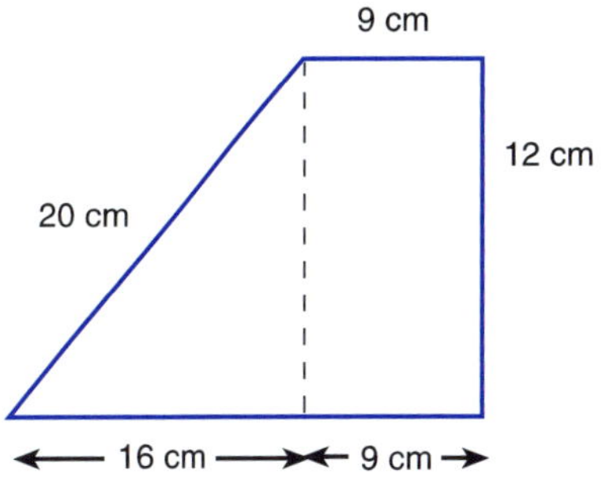

(a) Perimeter = 4 + 7 + 4 + 7
= 22 cm

(b) Perimeter = 20 + 9 + 12 + 9 + 16
= 66 cm

Area of 2D shapes

This is the amount of space a 2D shape covers. Common units of area are mm^2, cm^2, m^2 etc.

Estimating areas of irregular shapes

Areas of irregular shapes can be estimated by counting the squares the shape covers.

Example

- Label the squares as you count them.
- Try to match up parts of squares to make a whole one.

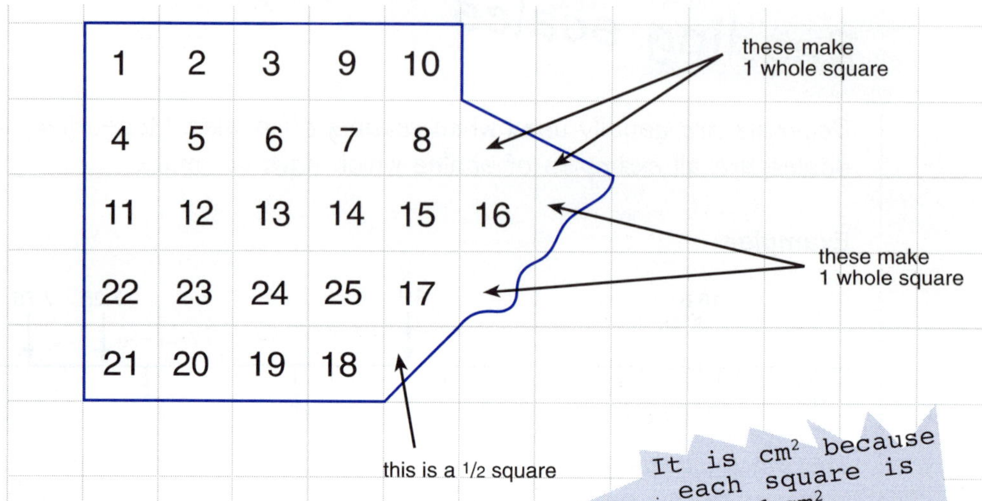

This shape has an area of $27\frac{1}{2}$ cm^2.

It is cm^2 because each square is 1 cm^2.

Using area formulae

You need to learn the formulae for the areas of rectangles and squares.

Area of a rectangle

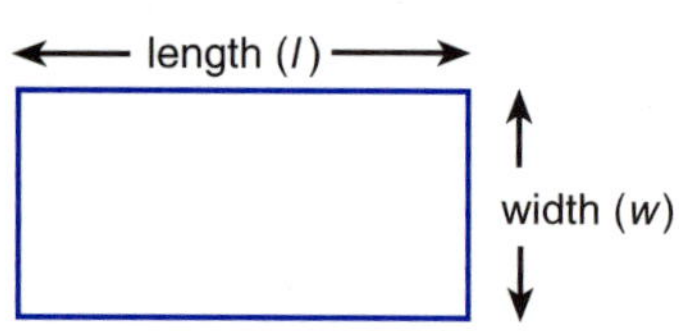

Area = length × width

$A = l \times w$

Area of a square

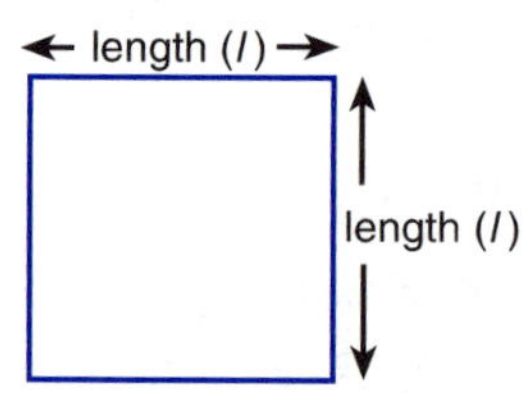

Area = length × length

$A = l \times l$

$A = l^2$

Area of a triangle

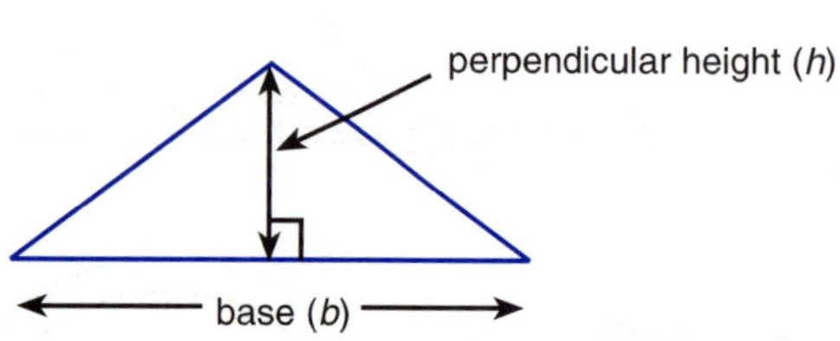

$A = \frac{1}{2} \times \text{base} \times \text{perpendicular height}$

$A = \frac{1}{2} \times b \times h$

Remember perpendicular height just means the height which is at 90° to the base.

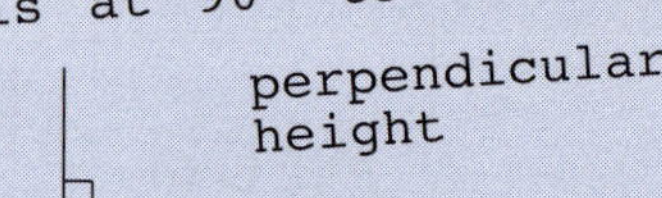

The perpendicular height is the same as the vertical height.

Examples

Find the areas of the following shapes.

(a)

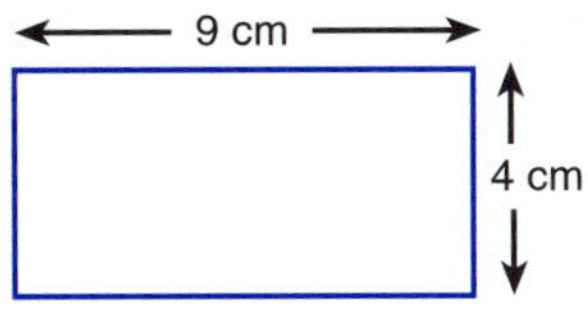

Don't forget the units.

$A = l \times w$

$= 9 \times 4$

$= 36\text{ cm}^2$

(b)

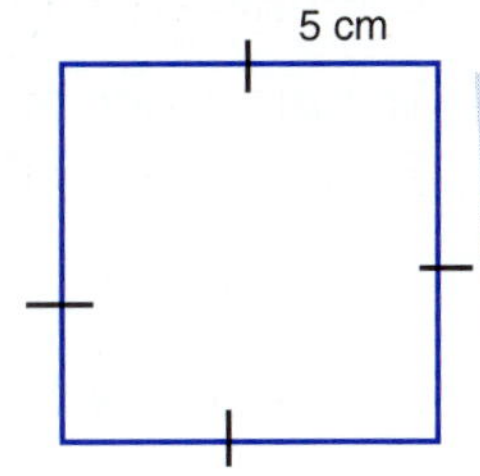

All the sides are the same so it is a square of length 5 cm.

Area = length × length

$A = l \times l$

$A = 5 \times 5$

$= 25\text{ cm}^2$

Marks are awarded for showing working out; don't just write the answer.

(c)

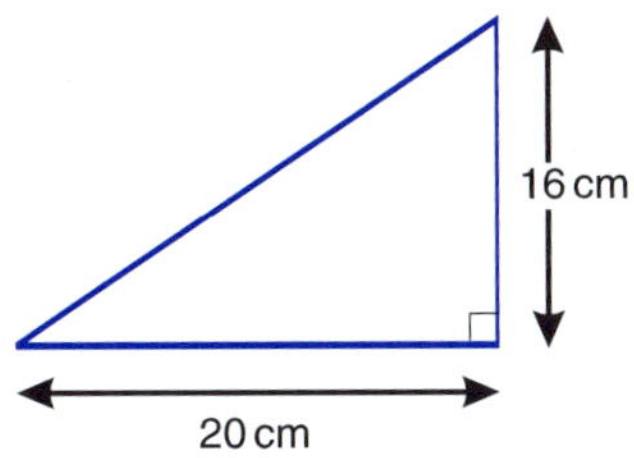

Use your calculator when working out areas.

Area $= \frac{1}{2} \times b \times h$

$A = \frac{1}{2} \times 20 \times 16$

$= 160\text{ cm}^2$

This could also be worked out as (16 × 20) ÷ 2.

Areas of more complicated shapes

When a shape is more complicated, split it up into simple shapes.

Example

Find the area of this shape.

Split a complex shape into simple ones and find the area of each part.

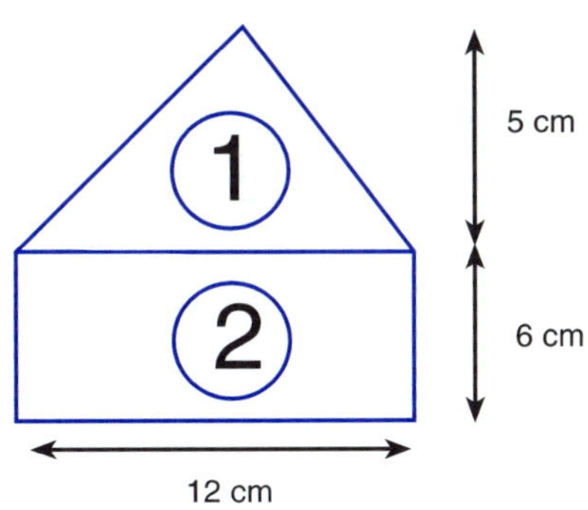

Area of ① $= \frac{1}{2} \times b \times h$

$= \frac{1}{2} \times 12 \times 5$

$= 30\text{ cm}^2$

Area of ② $= b \times h$

$= 12 \times 6$

$= 72\text{ cm}^2$

Total area = area of ① + area of ②

$= 30 + 72$

$= 102\text{ cm}^2$

Circumference and area of a circle

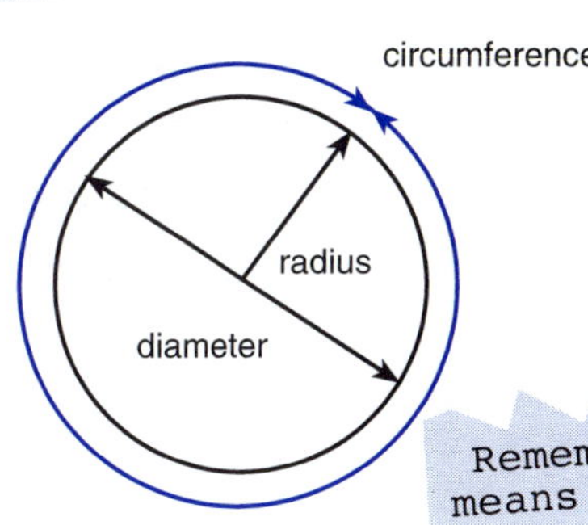

Circumference $= \pi \times \text{diameter} = \pi \times d$

$= 2 \times \pi \times \text{radius} = 2 \times \pi \times r$

Area $= \pi \times (\text{radius})^2 = \pi \times r^2$

Remember r^2 means $r \times r$.

Example

The diameter of a circular rose garden is 5 m.
Find the circumference and area of the garden. Use $\pi = 3.14$.

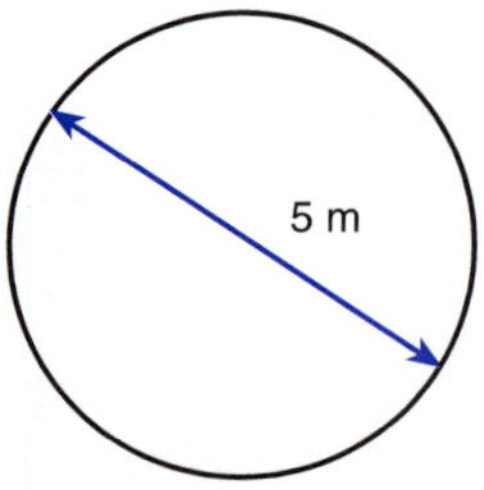

Make sure you use the value of π you are asked to use in the question.

$C = \pi \times d$ Choose the formula for circumference.

$= 3.14 \times 5$ Substitute in the values.

$= 15.7$ m

Remember that the circumference of a circle is the distance around the outside edge.

Diameter = 5, so radius = 5 ÷ 2 = 2.5 m.

$A = \pi \times r^2$ Work out the radius first.

$= 3.14 \times 2.5^2$ Remember 2.5^2 means 2.5×2.5.

$= 19.625$ m^2

Finding the radius and diameter of a circle given its circumference or area

Example

A circular fish-pond has a circumference of 12 m. Work out the length of the diameter to 1 d.p. Use $\pi = 3.14$.

$C = \pi \times d$

$12 = 3.14 \times d$ Substitute the known values into the formula.

$\frac{12}{3.14} = d$ Divide both sides by π (3.14).

So $d = 3.8216 \ldots$

$d = 3.8$ m (1 d.p.) Round the answer to 1 d.p. as instructed in the question.

Work out this type of question very carefully and remember to show full working out.

Example

A circular flower bed has an area of 1256 m^2. Work out its radius. Use $\pi = 3.14$.

$A = \pi \times r^2$

$1256 = 3.14 \times r^2$ Substitute values into the formula.

$\frac{1256}{3.14} = r^2$ Divide both sides by 3.14.

$r^2 = 400$ Since $r \times r = 400$ then $r = \sqrt{400}$.

$r = \sqrt{400}$ Take the square root of 400.

$r = 20$ m

Volume of 3D shapes

This is the amount of space a 3D shape occupies. Common units of volume are mm^3, cm^3, m^3.

Estimating volumes of 3D shapes

The volume of a 3D shape can be found by counting the number of $1cm^3$ cubes.

Example

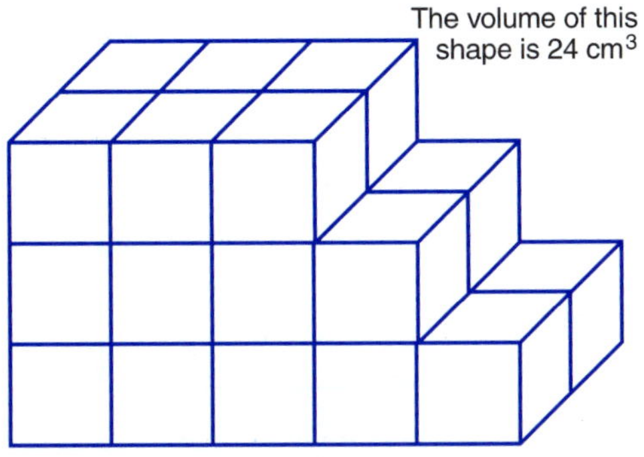

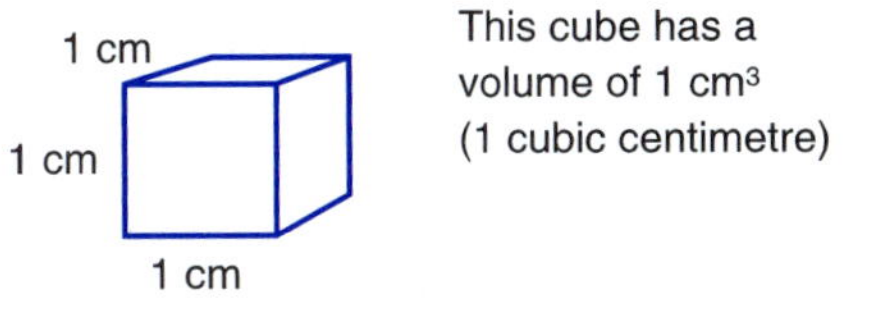

Using volume formulae

Volume of a cuboid

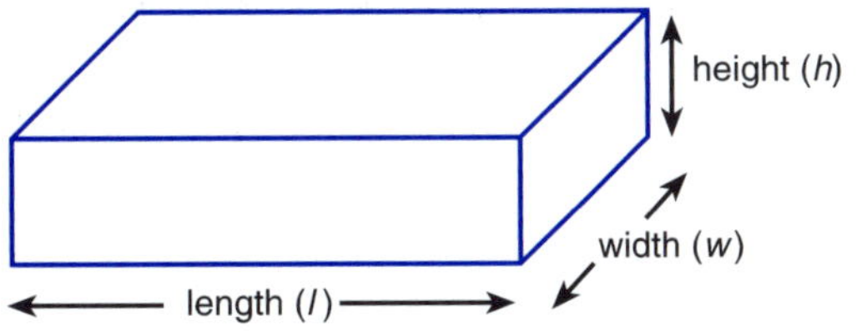

Volume = length × width × height

$V = l \times w \times h$

Volume of a cube

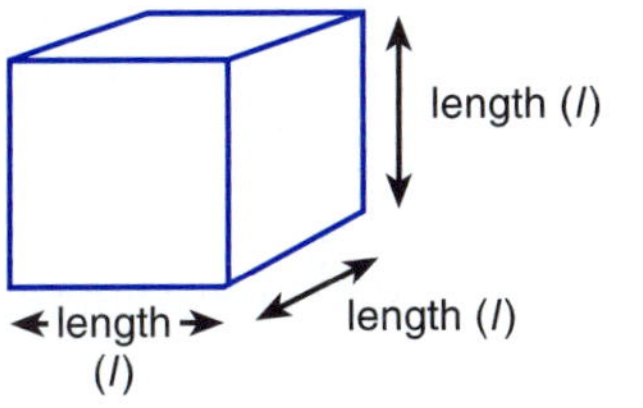

Volume = length × length × length

$V = l \times l \times l$

$V = l^3$

Example

Find the volume of the following shapes.

(a)

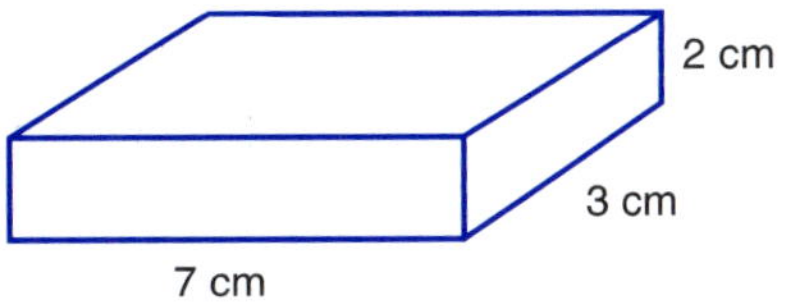

Volume = $l \times w \times h$

$= 7 \times 3 \times 2$

$= 42\ cm^3$

(b)

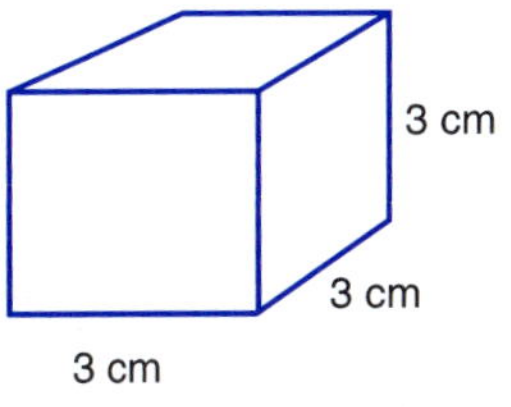

Volume = $l \times l \times l$

$= 3 \times 3 \times 3$

$= 27\ cm^3$

Measures
Questions

1 Approximately how many pounds are in a 2 kg bag of sugar?

2 Change 3500 g into kg.

3 Change 5 litres into ml.

4 Change 16 km into miles.

5 Change 5 inches into cm.

6 What do the pointers on the scales represent?

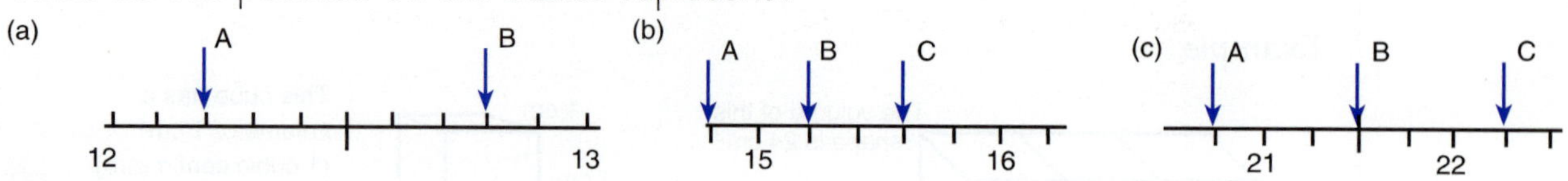

7 Work out the area of these shapes.

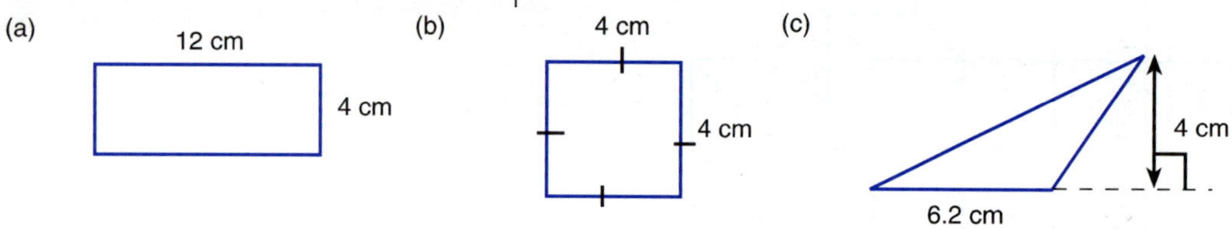

8 (a) What is the perimeter of this shape?

(b) What is the area of this shape?

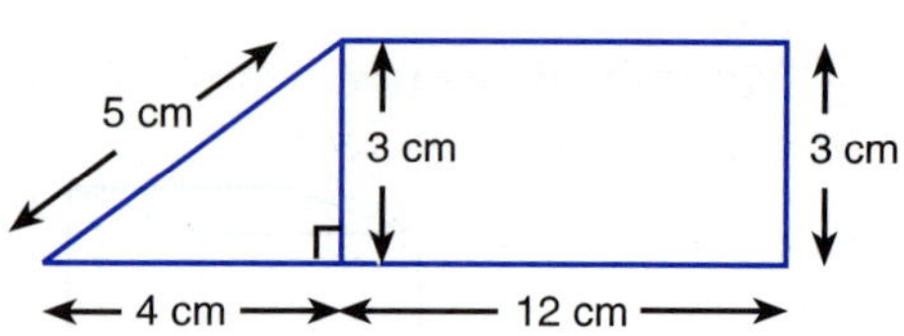

9 Work out the volume of these solids.

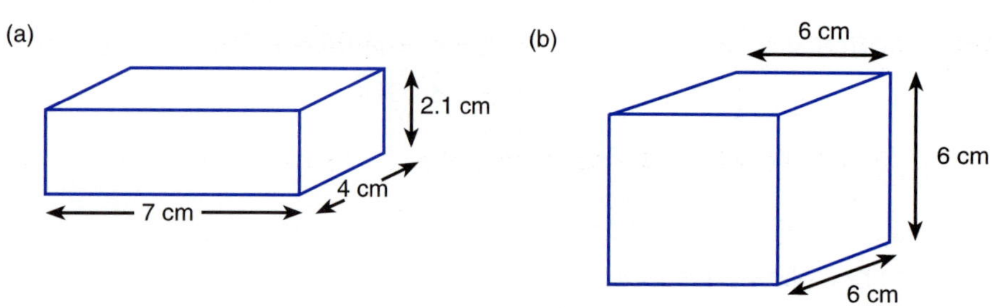

Handling data

Processing and interpreting data

Types of data

Examiner's tips and your notes

Quantitative – the answer is a number; for example 'How many blue cars are in the car park?'

Qualitative – the answer is a word; for example 'What is your favourite colour?'

Discrete data – each category is separate. Such data are often found by counting; for example the number of people with brown eyes, or with blue eyes.

Continuous data – here the values change from one category to the next. Such data are often found by measuring. Examples include the heights and weights of year 10 pupils.

Experiments and questionnaires

Data can be collected by carrying out experiments or by conducting surveys using questionnaires.

A **hypothesis** is a prediction which can be tested. An example is 'a six comes up more often than a five when a die is thrown 200 times'.

When designing **experiments** to test a hypothesis, make sure that there is no **bias**. For example, if a die is being thrown then it must be **fair**.

Questionnaires

When designing questionnaires:

- Decide what needs to be found out; that is the '**hypotheses**'.
- Give instructions on how the questionnaire has to be filled in.
- Do not ask for information which is not needed; for example, the person's name.
- Make the questions clear and concise.
- Keep the questionnaire short.
- If people's opinion is needed, make sure that your opinion is not evident. For example, do not ask a question like 'Do you agree that a leisure centre should have a tennis court rather than a squash court?' because it is obvious that you are in favour of a tennis court.
- Allow for any possible answers; for example:

  How many hours (to the nearest hour) a day do you watch TV?

  0–2 ☐ 3–5 ☐ 6–8 ☐ more than 8 ☐

Word any questions you write very carefully.

Collecting information

Data which has been collected can be sorted by putting it into a table known as a **tally chart** or **frequency table**. The tally chart shows the frequency of each item (how often the item occurs).

A **tally** is just a line. Tallies are often grouped into fives to make them easier to count. The fifth one forms a 'gate': ~~||||~~.

Example

Here are 40 pupils' marks out of 10 for a multiplication tables test.

6	2	9	9	9	2	4	5	4	10	6	4	4	3	8	7	7	1	10	10
4	7	5	3	8	1	7	5	9	7	4	3	3	2	8	8	9	4	5	9

Putting the results in a frequency table gives:

Take care that everything is counted.

Always check that the total frequencies add up to the number of items you started with.

The frequency is found by counting up the tallies in each group.

Mark	Tally	Frequency
0		0
1	||	2
2	|||	3
3	||||	4
4	~~||||~~ ||	7
5	||||	4
6	||	2
7	~~||||~~	5
8	||||	4
9	~~||||~~ |	6
10	|||	3
		Total 40

Grouping data

Discrete data

If the data cover a large range of results it is usual to group the data into **class intervals**. The class intervals have to be the same width.

Example

In an ice skating contest the marks awarded were:

12	5	14	13	22	22	21	25	9
12	9	23	24	3	6	27	17	4
27	27	7	4	3	17	7	21	18
7	1	20	18	2	20	19	22	

- The data have been grouped into class intervals of 5 in the table.
- Choose sensible groupings of 2, 5, and 10.
- Check that all the data have been included.

It helps if you cross off each number as you put it in the table.

Mark	Tally	Frequency
0–4	𝍸 I	6
5–9	𝍸 II	7
10–14	IIII	4
15–19	𝍸	5
20–24	𝍸 IIII	9
25–29	IIII	4
		Total 35

Continuous data

For continuous data, it is best to put the results into class intervals. The class intervals are often written using **inequalities**.

Example

The weight of 30 people in a factory:

Weight (kg)	Frequency
$45 \leq W < 55$	7
$55 \leq W < 65$	13
$65 \leq W < 75$	6
$75 \leq W < 85$	4
	30

$45 \leq W < 55$ is called a **class interval** – notice that the class intervals are all equal in width.

$55 \leq W < 65$ means the weights are between 55 and 65 kg. $55 \leq W$ means the weight is **greater than or equal to 55 kg**. $W < 65$ means the weight is **less than** 65 kg. 65 kg would be included in the next group.

Displaying data

Data can be presented in several ways using different types of diagrams.

Bar charts

Make sure that you draw the bars the same width.

A bar chart is a set of bars or columns of equal width. They show the important features of a set of results. The height of each bar is used to show the frequency. There should be gaps between the bars. The gaps should be as narrow as possible.

Qualitative data are usually illustrated using bar charts.

Example

The bar chart illustrates the marks obtained in a multiplication tables test.

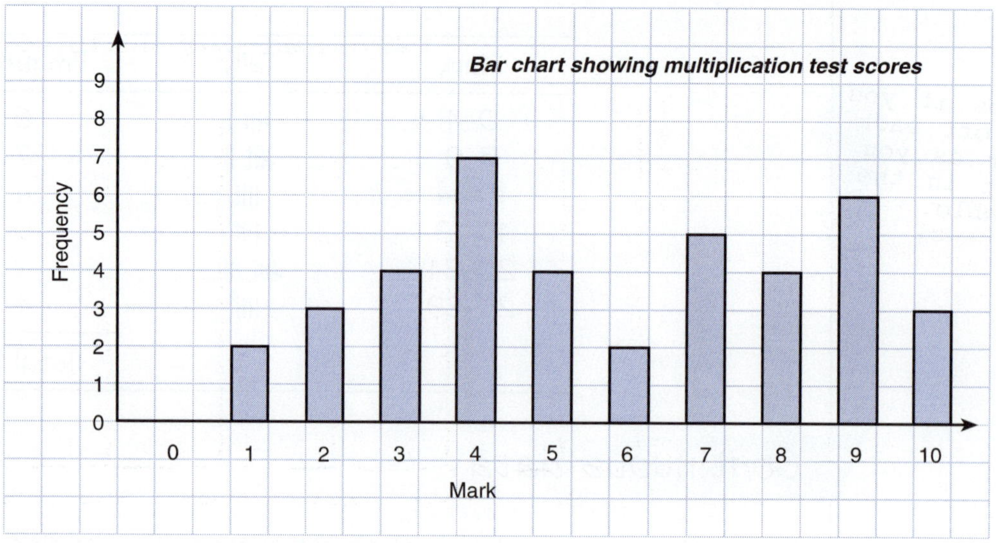

Make sure that the horizontal and vertical axes are clearly labelled.
The scales are chosen such that the bar chart is a sensible size.

Bar charts of **grouped data** are drawn in a similar way.

Example

The bar chart illustrates the marks awarded in an ice skating contest.

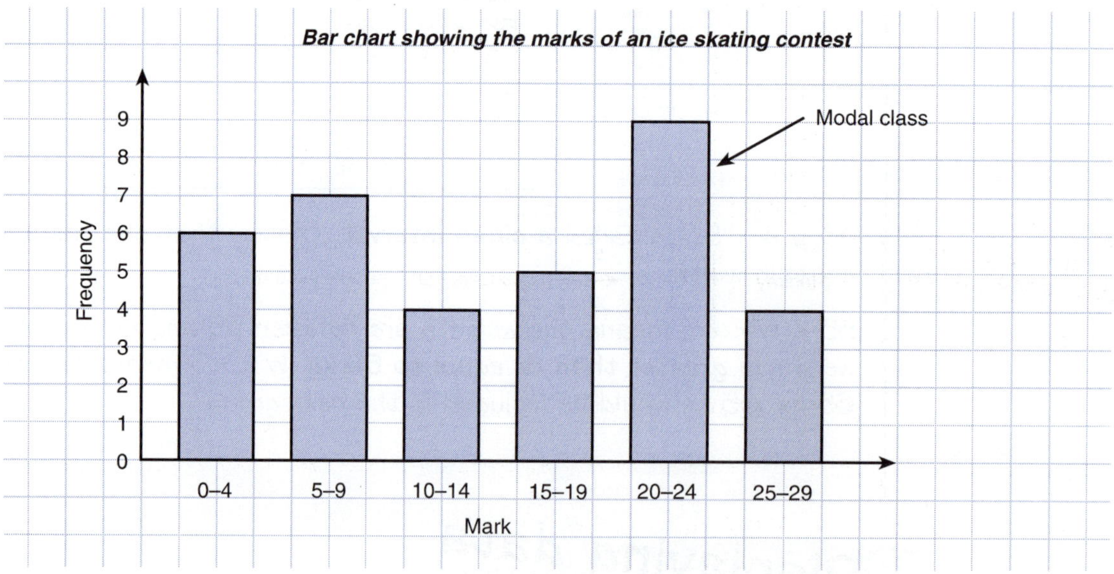

The **modal class** is 20–24 because this group has the greatest frequency.

Bar line graphs

These are similar to bar charts except only a line is drawn. They are used for **discrete data**.

Check that you have labelled the axes!

Example

The bar line graph shows the results of a survey on pupils' favourite colours.

From the diagram it can be seen that 9 people liked red.

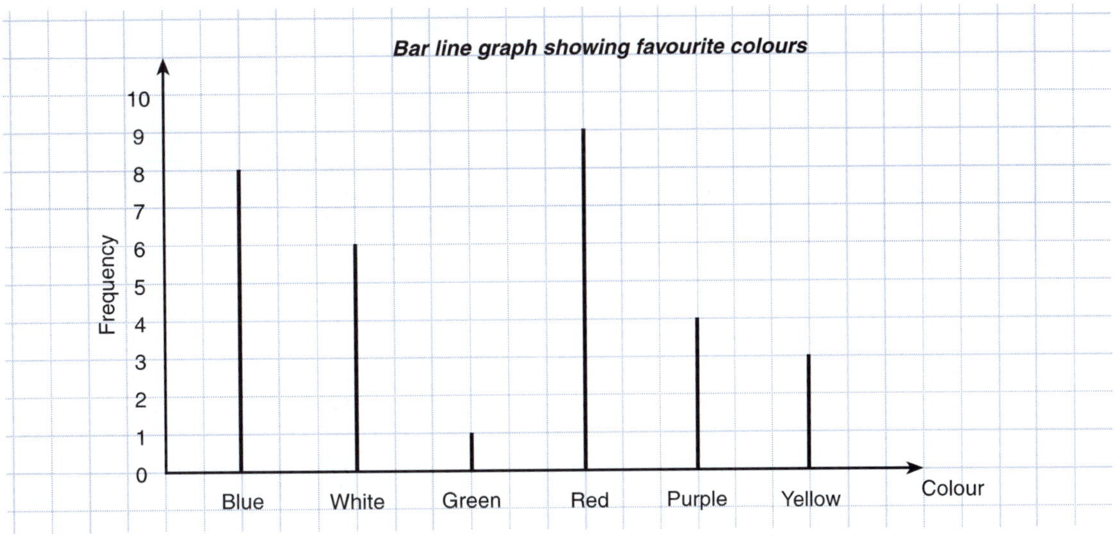

Pictograms

Pictograms use symbols where each symbol represents a certain number of items.

Example

The pictogram represents the leisure activities of year 8 pupils.

Draw your symbols carefully. They must all be the same size.

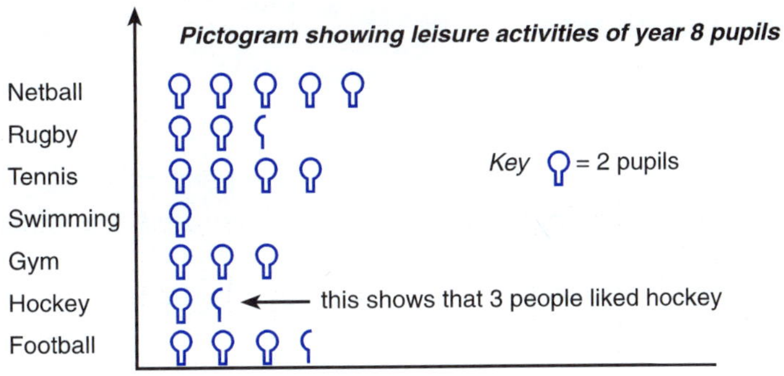

Half a bat stands for one person.

- Put a label at the side of each row.
- Each symbol must be the same size, with equal gaps between them.
- Write a title and a key.

Pie charts

These are circles split into sections, each representing a certain number of items.

Calculating angles for a pie chart

- Find the total for the items listed.
- Find the fraction of the total for each item.
- Multiply the fraction by 360° to find the angle.

Remember there are 360° at the centre of a circle.

You will need a protractor and a pair of compasses for pie chart questions.

Example

The table gives the hair colour of 24 ten-year-olds.

Hair colour	Frequency
Brown	8
Auburn	4
Blonde	6
Black	6
	Total = 24

8 out of 24 have brown hair, so $\frac{8}{24} \times 360° = 120°$

fraction — multiply by 360°

Key in on the calculator:

8 ÷ 24 × 360 =

Check that the angles add up to 360°.

Auburn $\frac{4}{24} \times 360° = 60°$

Blonde $\frac{6}{24} \times 360° = 90°$

Black $\frac{6}{24} \times 360° = 90°$

Total = 360°

Pie chart showing hair colour

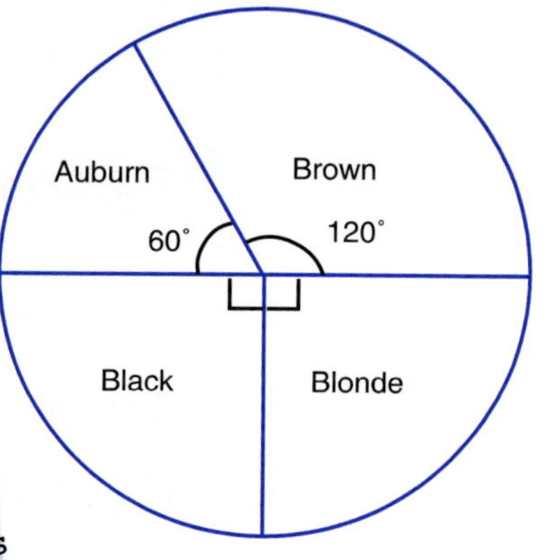

Remember to name the sectors and measure the angles carefully with a protractor.

Interpreting pie charts

Example

The pie chart shows how some year 10 pupils spent Saturday night. If 140 pupils went to the ice rink, how many went to the disco and the cinema?

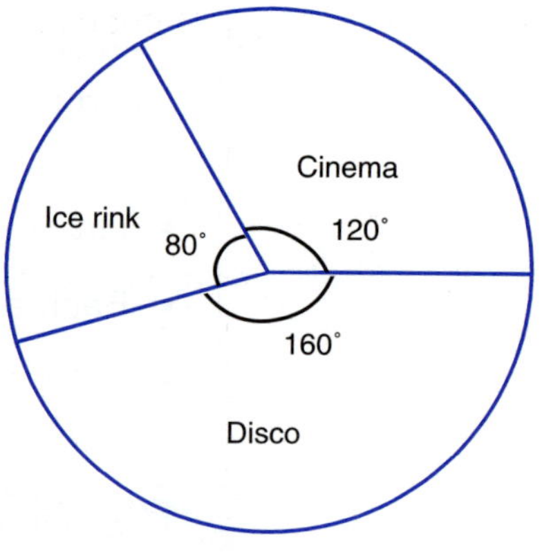

Check that your answers seem sensible.

80° represents 140 pupils. Work out 1°.

1° represents $\frac{140}{80°} = 1.75$

Number at disco = 160° × 1.75 = 280 pupils

Number at cinema = 120° × 1.75 = 210 pupils

Line graphs

These are a set of points joined by a line. Line graphs can be used to show **continuous data**.

Example

Year	1988	1989	1990	1991	1992	1993	1994	1995	1996
School roll	729	805	920	860	750	690	790	870	940

The **middle values** (for example, point A) have no meaning. Point A does not mean that halfway between 1991 and 1992 there were 800 pupils on the school roll.

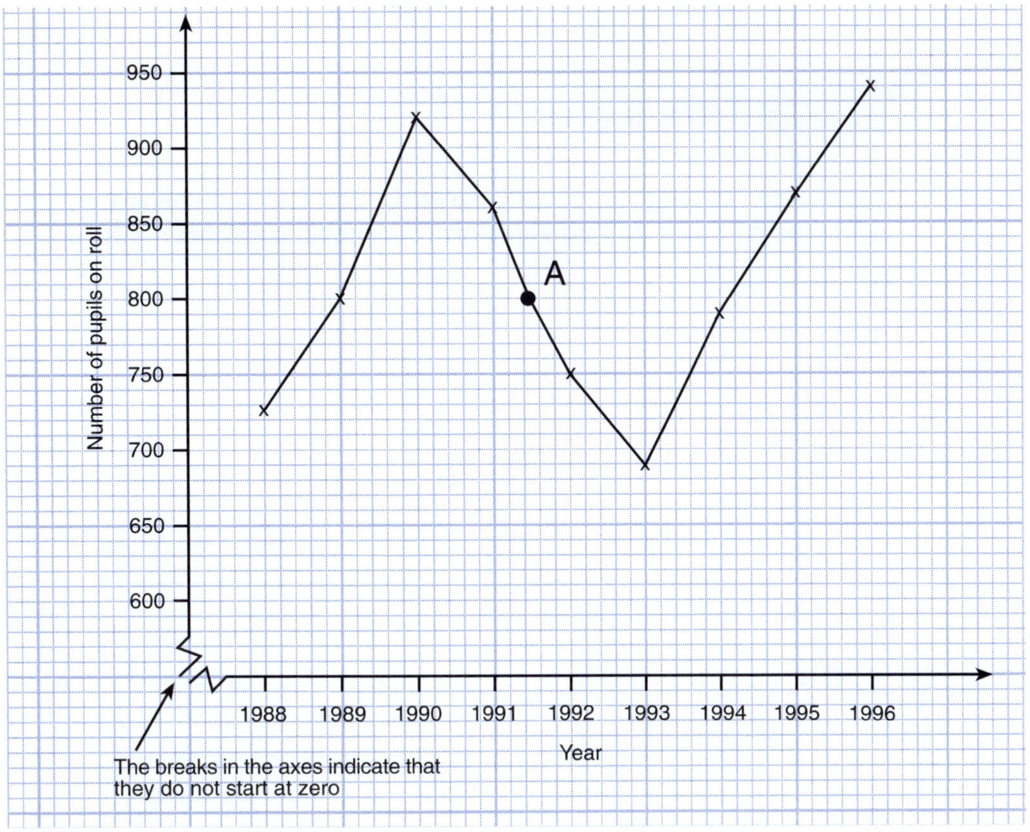

Frequency polygons

These are used to join the **midpoints** of class intervals for grouped or continuous data.

Example

Consider the bar chart showing the marks of an ice skating contest.

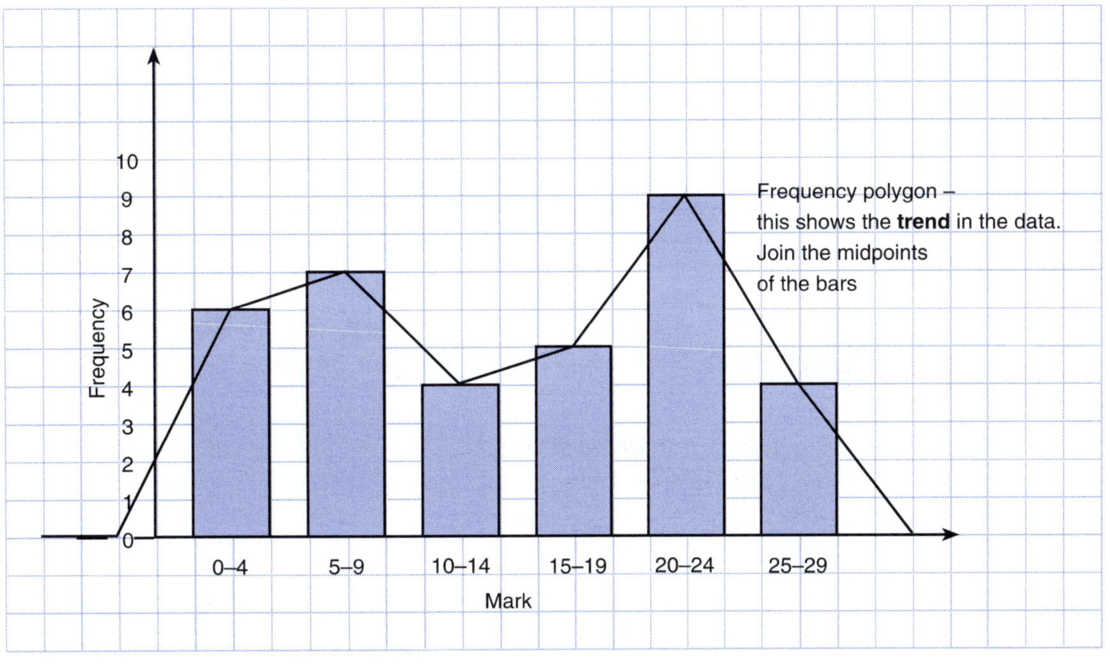

For a frequency polygon remember to plot at the midpoint of the class interval.

- To draw the frequency polygon: put a cross on the middle of each bar;
- join up the points with a ruler, and continue the lines down to the x axis before the first bar and after the last bar.

Scatter diagrams

A scatter diagram (**scattergraph**) is used to show two sets of data at the same time. It shows the **correlation** (connection) between two sets of data.

There are three types of correlation: **positive**, **negative** or **zero**.

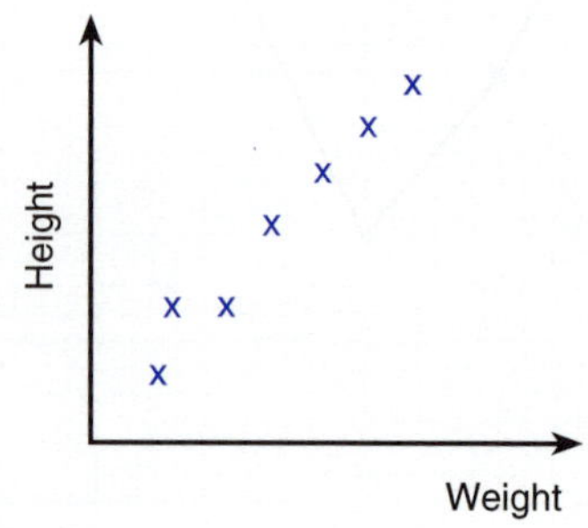

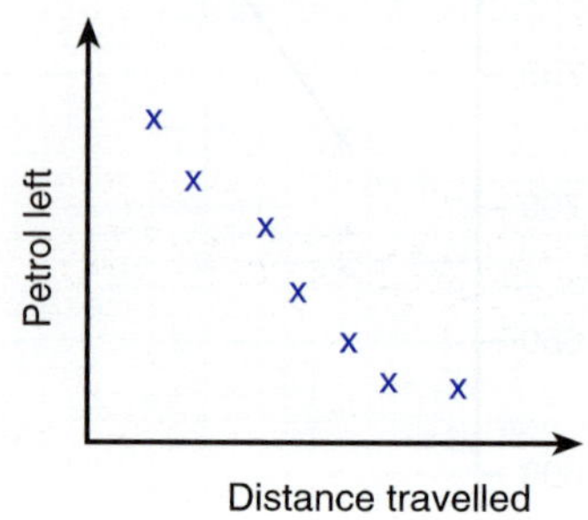

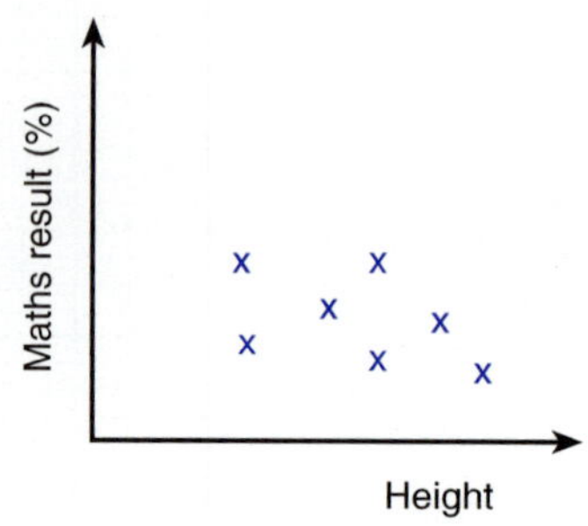

Positive – this is when both variables are increasing. If the points are nearly a straight line, it is said to have a **high positive correlation**.

Negative – this is when one variable increases whilst the other decreases. The one above has a **high negative correlation**.

Zero – this is when there is little or no correlation between the variables.

Drawing a scatter diagram

- Work out the scales first.
- Plot the points carefully.
- Each time a point is plotted, tick it off.

Example

Ten pupils sat two maths papers. Their results are as follows:

Maths paper 1	79	52	61	73	12	96	79	37	42	86
Maths paper 2	68	45	58	75	18	89	79	39	38	88

For the first set of data plot 79 across and 68 up.

Do not rush when drawing a scatter diagram, otherwise you will plot the points incorrectly.

The scatter diagram shows that there is a **positive correlation**. In general if the pupils did well on paper 1 they did well on paper 2.

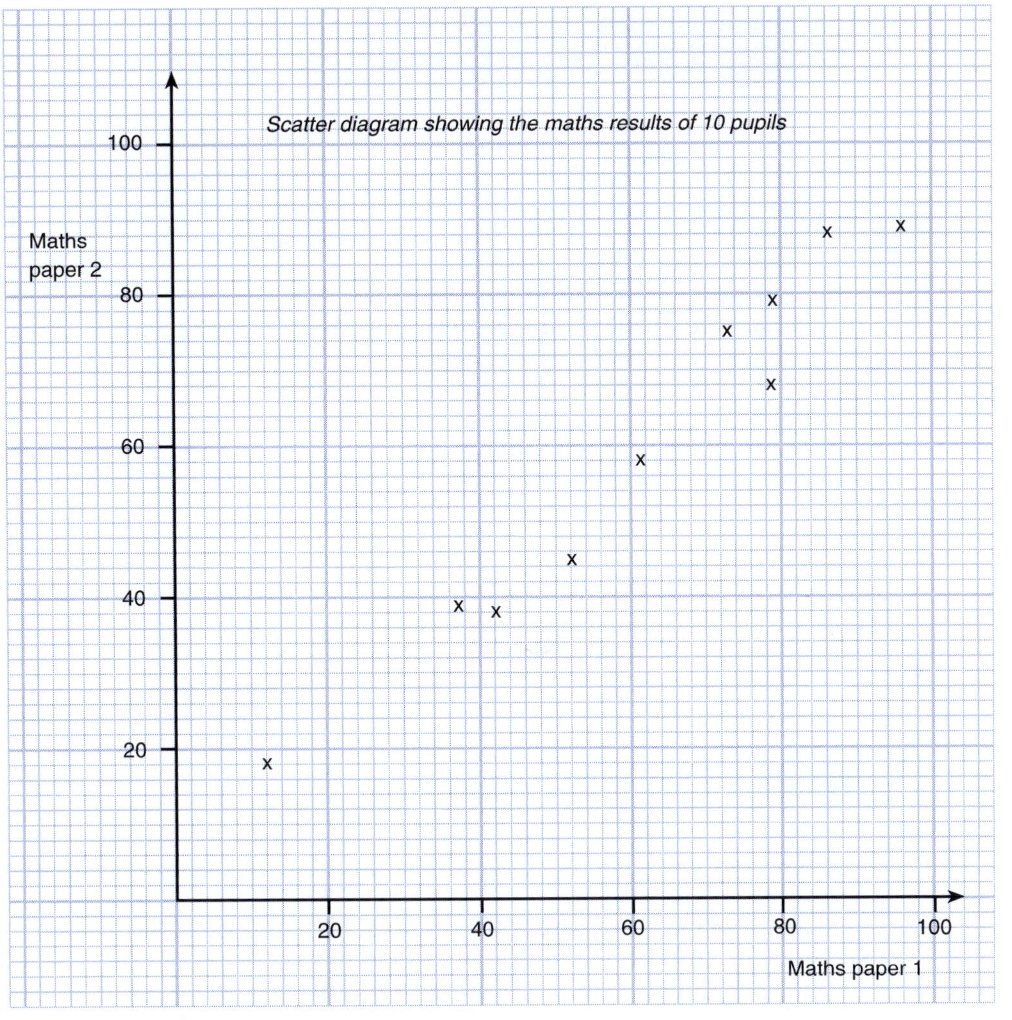

Misleading graphs

Statistical graphs are sometimes presented in a misleading way; they do not tell the true story.

Graphs without a scale

This graph is trying to show that Superbrand is better than brands A, B and C. Since there are no scales the graph is meaningless. The Superbrand column is twice as wide as the others. The graph is trying to 'trick' you into buying the product.

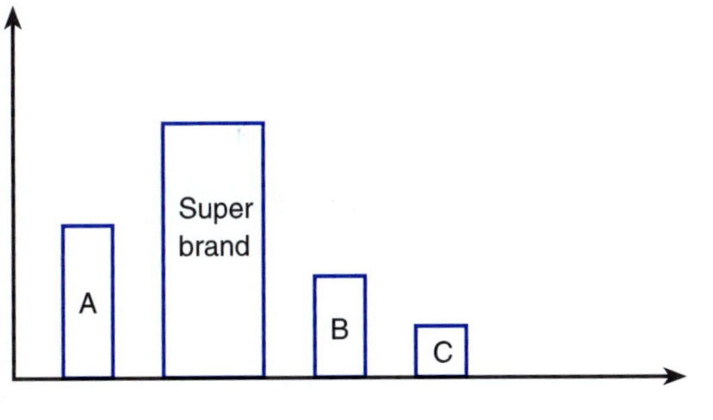

Scales that do not start at zero

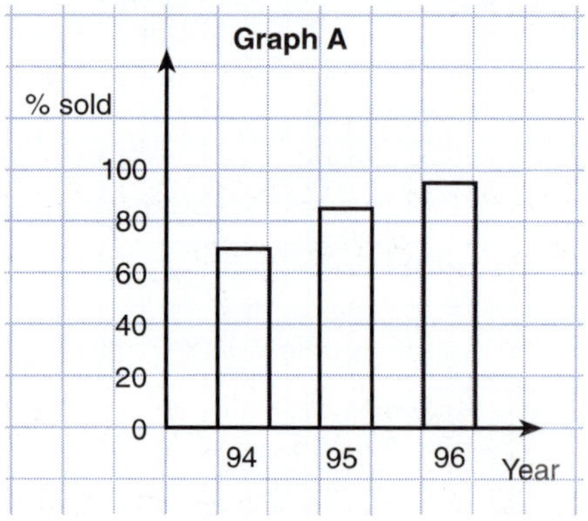

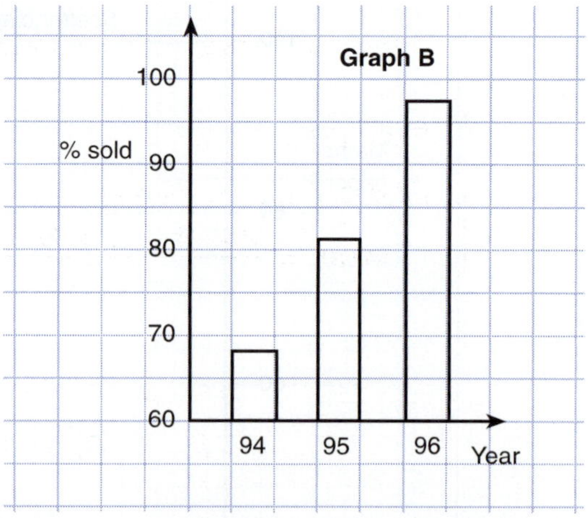

In the exam make your criticisms clear and concise.

In Graph A, the scale starts at zero and shows a steady growth in sales.

In Graph B, the scale starts at a higher value and gives the impression that there has been lots of growth in sales – it is **misleading**.

Misleading pictograms

Misleading pictograms occur when the size of the picture changes.

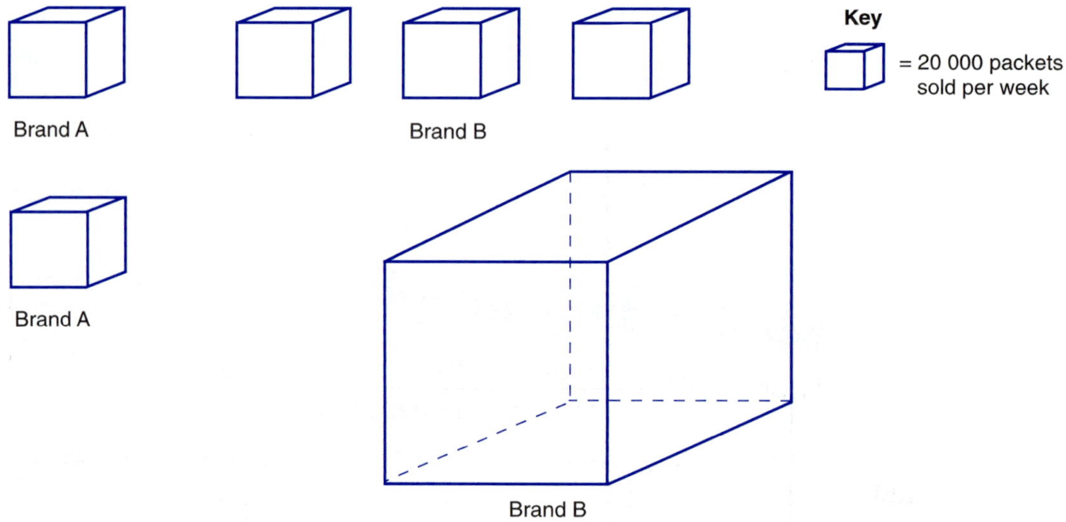

Beware if the pictures are not the same size.

Brand A sells 20 000 packets a week. Brand B sells 60 000 packets a week. If instead of drawing Brand B's sales as three boxes, Box A was made three times bigger the impression is given that Brand B sold much more than 60 000 packets.

Averages and spread

There are three types of averages:

- **Mean** – sometimes known as 'the average'. It is calculated as the sum of a set of values divided by the number of values used.
- **Median** – the middle value when the numbers are put in order of size.

- **Mode** – the value that occurs the most often.

The **range** tells you the **spread** of information:

Range = highest value – lowest value

Example

Find the mean, median, mode and range of 2, 9, 3, 6, 4, 4, 5, 8, 4.

$$\text{Mean} = \frac{2+9+3+6+4+4+5+8+4}{9} = \frac{45}{9} = 5$$

Median 2, 3, 4, 4, 4, 5, 6, 8, 9 Put in order of size first.

~~2~~, ~~3~~, ~~4~~, ~~4~~, (4), ~~5~~, ~~6~~, ~~8~~, ~~9~~ Cross off from the end to find the middle value.

Mode = 4 as it occurs 3 times.

Range = 9 – 2 = 7

highest lowest

If there are two numbers in the middle, the median is halfway between them.

Remember to subtract the two values in order to obtain the range.

Finding averages from a frequency table

A frequency table tells us **how many** are in a group.

Example

Number of goals (x)	0	1	2	3	4	5
Frequency (f)	6	4	7	2	3	1

This tells us that six teams got zero goals.

Two teams got three goals.

Mean

$$\text{Mean} = \frac{\text{total of the results when multiplied}}{\text{total of the frequency}}$$

$$= \frac{(6 \times 0) + (4 \times 1) + (7 \times 2) + (2 \times 3) + (3 \times 4) + (1 \times 5)}{6+4+7+2+3+1}$$

$$= \frac{0+4+14+6+12+5}{23}$$

$$= \frac{41}{23} = 1.78 \text{ (2 d.p.) goals per team.}$$

Remember to add up the total frequency.

Median

Write out the data:

0, 0, 0, 0, 0, 0, 1, 1, 1, 1, 2, 2, 2, 2, 2, 2, 2, 3, 3, 4, 4, 4, 5

12th goal 3 teams got 4 goals

The middle number of goals is the 12th value, 2.

A quicker way to find the median is to find the 12th value in the frequency table.

Number of goals	0	1	2
Frequency	6	4	7

the first 10 values   12th value is in here

Remember to write down the answer 2, not the frequency 7.

Median number of goals is 2.

Mode

This is the one that has the highest frequency.

Mode = 2 goals because it has a frequency higher than any others.

Range

Range = highest score – lowest score
= 5 – 0
= 5 goals

Comparing sets of data

The range and averages are used to compare sets of data.

Example

Class 8M obtained a mean of 68% in a test.

Class 8U obtained a mean of 87% in the same test.

From these averages we would say 8U's results are better than 8M's. However, if we look at the range:

Use the range when comparing data.

Class 8M range = 100% – 22% = 78%
Class 8U range = 93% – 81% = 12%

Using the range it can be seen that not all of 8U's results are better than 8M's, because some of 8M obtained higher marks than 8U. The average for 8M has been lowered because of the low marks achieved by some pupils.

Processing and interpreting data

Questions

1 The frequency table shows the hair colour of 20 pupils.

Hair colour	Brown	Black	Auburn	Blonde
Frequency	9	6	3	2

Draw a pictogram of the information.

Let  represent 2 pupils.

2 The pie chart shows the favourite subjects of 720 girls.

(a) How many girls like maths?

(b) How many girls like art?

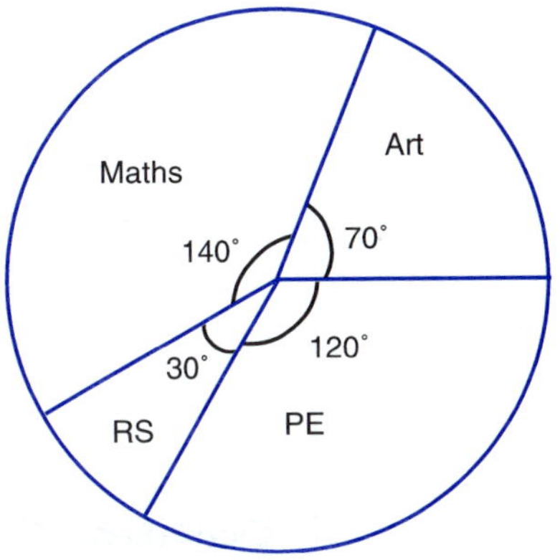

3 What type of correlation does the scatter diagram show?

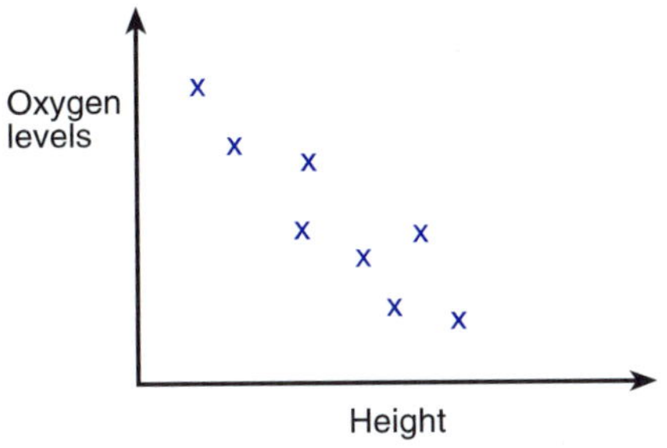

4 Explain why this graph is misleading.

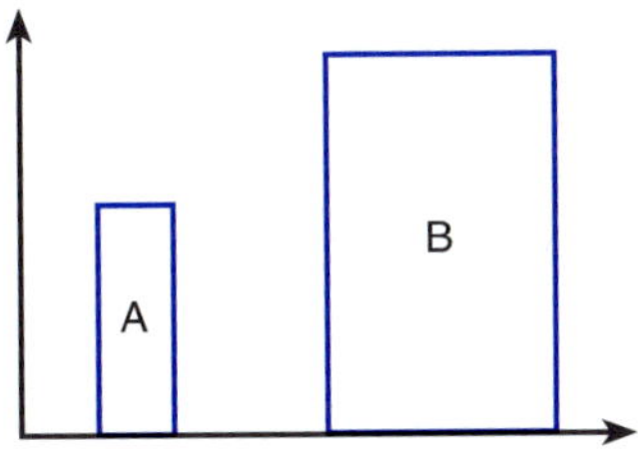

5 For the set of data 2, 7, 9, 13, 2, 4, 1, 2, 2, 5 find:

(a) the mean (b) the median (c) the mode (d) the range

6 This question was found on a questionnaire: 'Do you agree that *Neighbours* is better than *Home and Away*?' Why is this not a very good question?

Estimating and calculating the probabilities of events

Probability

Examiner's tips and your notes

Probability is the chance or likelihood that something will happen.

Probabilities must be written as a **fraction**, **decimal** or **percentage**.

All probabilities lie between 0 and 1. No event has a probability greater than 1.

If you get a probability greater than 1 you must be wrong, so check again!

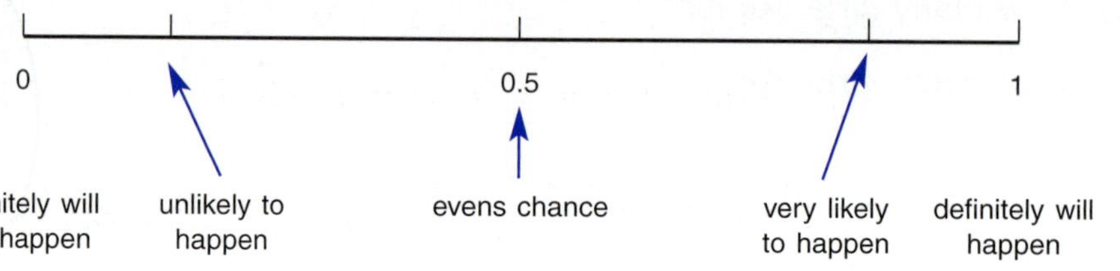

Examples

'I will grow to 9 metres tall' is an event which will **definitely not happen** so has a probability of **zero**.

'I will die' is an event that **definitely will happen**, so it has a probability of **one**.

Exhaustive events account for all possible outcomes. For example, the list 1, 2, 3, 4, 5, 6 gives all possible outcomes when a fair die is thrown.

Mutually exclusive events are events which cannot happen at the same time. For example two students are chosen at random.

Event A – one student has brown hair.
Event B – one student wears glasses.

These events are **not mutually exclusive** because brown haired students could wear glasses.

Probability of an event = $\dfrac{\textbf{number of ways an event can happen}}{\textbf{total number of outcomes}}$

P(event) is a shortened way of writing the probability of an event.

Example

There are 3 red, 2 white and 4 yellow beads in a bag. Audrey picks out a bead at random from the bag. What is the probability that she picks:

(a) a red bead, (b) a yellow bead, (c) a white bead,

(d) a green bead, (e) a red, white or yellow bead?

Remember probabilities must be written as a fraction, decimal or percentage.

(a) P(red) = $\frac{3}{9}$ ← these are the number of red beads; ← there are nine possible outcomes

(b) P(yellow) = $\frac{4}{9}$

(c) P(white) = $\frac{2}{9}$

(d) P(green) = $\frac{0}{9}$

There are no green beads in the bag. This event will definitely not happen.

(e) P(red, white or yellow) = $\frac{9}{9} = 1$

All probabilities add up to 1, i.e. choosing a red, white or yellow will definitely happen.

Example

A bag of sweets contains 4 eclairs, 5 mints and 2 caramels. Fiona picks out a sweet at random from the bag. Write as a fraction, decimal and a percentage the probability that she chooses:

(a) an eclair (b) a mint

Remember to change $\frac{4}{11}$ into a decimal.

(a) P(eclair) = $\frac{4}{11} = 0.\dot{3}\dot{6} = 36.\dot{3}\dot{6}\%$

(b) P(mint) = $\frac{5}{11} = 0.\dot{4}\dot{5} = 45.\dot{4}\dot{5}\ \%$

Divide 4 by 11, then multiply by 100% to change it into a percentage.

Probability of an event not happening

If there are two events which are mutually exclusive:

P(event will happen) = 1 − P(event will not happen)

P(event will not happen) = 1 − P(event will happen)

Example

The probability of getting a 6 when a die is thrown is $\frac{1}{6}$.

The probability of not getting a 6 is $\frac{5}{6}$. (There are 5 ways of not getting a 6 [1, 2, 3, 4, 5]. There are 6 outcomes on the die.)

P(not a 6) = 1 − P(6) = $1 - \frac{1}{6} = \frac{5}{6}$

Example

The probability that somebody gets flu next winter is 0.42. What is the probability that they do not get flu next winter?

P(not get flu) = 1 − P(get flu) = 1 − 0.42 = 0.58

Expected number

Example

Remember there are 6 outcomes on a die.

If a die is thrown 300 times, approximately how many fives are likely to be obtained?

P(5) = $\frac{1}{6} \times 300 = 50$ fives

Key in the calculator: 1 [÷] 6 [×] 300 [=]

A 5 is expected $\frac{1}{6}$ of the time.

Example

The probability of passing a driving test at the first attempt is 0.65. If there are 200 people taking a test for the first time, how many would you expect to pass it?

0.65 × 200 = 130 people

Relative frequencies

If a die is thrown 180 times it would be expected that about 30 twos would be thrown, $\frac{1}{6} \times 180 = 30$.

Experiments are often used to estimate probabilities. This is called the **relative frequency** that the event will happen.

Example

A die is thrown 180 times and the frequency of a score of 2 is recorded every 30 throws.

Number of throws	Total frequency of 2s	Relative frequency
30	3	0.1
60	7	0.12
90	16	0.18
120	19	0.16
150	24	0.16
180	31	0.17

This value is obtained by dividing the total frequency of 2s by the number of throws, e.g. $\frac{19}{120}$.

It is expected that $\frac{1}{6} = 0.1\dot{6} = 0.17$ of the throws will be 2s.

As the number of throws increases the relative frequency gets closer to the expected probability.

Relative frequency is used as an estimate of probability.

Relative frequency of an event = $\dfrac{\textbf{number of times the event occurred}}{\textbf{total number of trials}}$

Example

When a die was thrown 80 times a six came up 12 times. What is the relative frequency of getting a six?

Number of trials = 80

Number of sixes = 12

Relative frequency = $\frac{12}{80} = 0.15$

The **theoretical** probability = $\frac{1}{6} = 0.1\dot{6}$

If it is not possible to calculate probability an experiment is used to find the relative frequency. In some real life situations the probabilities may not be equal. For example:

- the probability of winning, losing or drawing a game may not be $\frac{1}{3}$ each;
- the probability of passing or failing a test may not be $\frac{1}{2}$ etc.

In these cases a **test** or **survey** may need to be carried out.

Possible outcomes for two events

Using tables is helpful when there are outcomes of two events. These tables are sometimes known as **sample space diagrams**.

Example

A die and a coin are thrown together. Represent the outcomes on a sample space diagram:

Coin						
Head	H1	H2	H3	H4	H5	H6
Tail	T1	T2	T3	T4	T5	T6
	1	2	3	4	5	6
			Die			

This means a head on the coin, a 6 on the die.

There are 12 **outcomes**.

Example

Two dice are thrown together and their scores are added. The diagram shows all the outcomes. Find the probability of a score of 7, and of a score that is a multiple of 3.

There are 36 outcomes.

P(score of 7) = $\frac{6}{36} = \frac{1}{6}$

P(multiple of 3) = $\frac{12}{36} = \frac{1}{3}$

To help: put a ring or square around the numbers you need.

Die 1						
6	7	8	9	10	11	12
5	6	7	8	9	10	11
4	5	6	7	8	9	10
3	4	5	6	7	8	9
2	3	4	5	6	7	8
1	2	3	4	5	6	7
	1	2	3	4	5	6
			Die 2			

2 on Die 1
6 on Die 2
2 + 6 = 8

Two-way tables

These are also used to show possible outcomes.

Example

The diagram shows a two-way table for pupils in a class, who are studying either French or German.

	Male	Female	Total
French	7	17	24
German	4	6	10
Total	11	23	34

(a) If a person is chosen at random, what is the probability they do French?

P(French) = $\frac{24}{34} = \frac{12}{17}$

(b) If a girl is chosen at random what is the probability she does German?

P(German) = $\frac{6}{23}$

6 girls do German

23 girls in total

Estimating and calculating the probabilities of events

Questions

1 Give an example of an event which has a probability of 1.

2 Give an example of two events which are mutually exclusive.

3 A bag has 3 red and 4 blue beads in it. Imran chooses a bead at random from the bag. What is the probability he chooses:

(a) a red bead, (b) a blue bead, (c) a green bead?

4 The spinner is spun once. What is the probability that the spinner lands on:

(a) a number 1, (b) an odd number, (c) a multiple of 3?

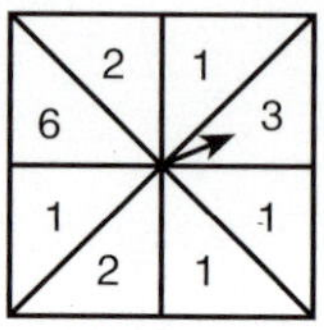

5 The probability that the bus is late is $\frac{7}{9}$. What is the probability it is not late?

6 The probability of getting a 'D' grade in maths is 0.32. If 300 people sit the exam, how many are expected to get a 'D'?

7 When a die was thrown 320 times a four came up 58 times. What is the relative frequency of getting a four?

8 Two dice are thrown together and their scores added.

(a) Fill in the table.

(b) What is the probability:

(i) the total score is 4,

(ii) the total score is odd?

Die 1						
6						12
5						
4		6				
3						
2			5			
1						7
	1	2	3	4	5	6
			Die 2			

Answers

Number and algebra

Place value and the number system

1 Two million, four hundred and sixty-two thousand, and four

2 (a) 60 (b) 90 (c) 150

3 (a) 1 300 (b) 600

4 (a) 6 000 (b) 8 000

5 6 °C

6 (a) 2 (b) −9 (c) −6

7 (a) $4 \times 4 \times 4 \times 4 \times 4 \times 4$ (b) $3 \times 3 \times 3 \times 3$

8 6×10^{15}

9 (a) $\frac{6}{27}$ (b) $\frac{3}{4}$

10 0.63, 4.07, 4.89, 6.43, 8.295, 8.31, 10.7

11 $\frac{17}{100}$

12 61%

13 (a) 2 : 3 (b) 3 : 1 (c) 2 : 1

14 (a) 0.8 (b) 80%

15 14.64

16 9.4

Relationships between numbers and computation methods

1 (a) 1, 3, 5, 7, 9, 11, 13, 15, 17, 19, 21, 23 (b) 2, 4, 6, 8, 10, 12, 14, 16, 18, 20, 22, 24 (c) 2, 3, 5, 7, 11, 13, 17, 19, 23 (d) 1, 4, 9, 16 (e) 7, 14, 21 (f) 1, 2, 4, 5, 10, 20

2 (a) 8 (b) 9

3 (a) 124 (b) 623 (c) 42 000 (d) 2.46
(e) 0.273 (f) 1 200 000

4 (a) 27 135 (b) 41 (Remember to show your working in full.)

5 (a) 30.39 (b) 6.28 (c) 126.3 (d) 20.8

6 (a) £8 (b) £10.92

7 43% (to nearest 1%)

8 £5 446

9 £105, £315

10 £2.84 (to nearest 1p)

11 (a) 22 (b) 24

12 $(60 \times 50) \div 30 = 100$

Solving numerical problems

1 Four pounds and sixty pence i.e. £4.60
2 x = 2.9 (to 1 d.p.)
3 No, it is 10 times too big
4 £215.13
5 £289
6 £81.57 (to nearest penny)
7 £7 459
8 2 400 French francs
9 4.5 km/h
10 1 635

Functional relationships

1 (a) $b - 8$ (b) $x + 12$ (c) $2p - 5$ (d) $\frac{h}{4}$
(e) $6 - p$ (f) $3x - h$
2 14
3 (a) 16.1 (b) 16 (c) 30 (d) 8.405 (e) 24.6
4 (a) 13, add 2 each time (b) −3, subtract 3 each time
(c) 80, multiply by 2 each time (d) 1, divide by 3 each time
(e) 48, add the two previous terms each time (f) 25, square numbers
5 (a) $U_n = 4n + 1$ (b) $U_n = 2n + 4$
6

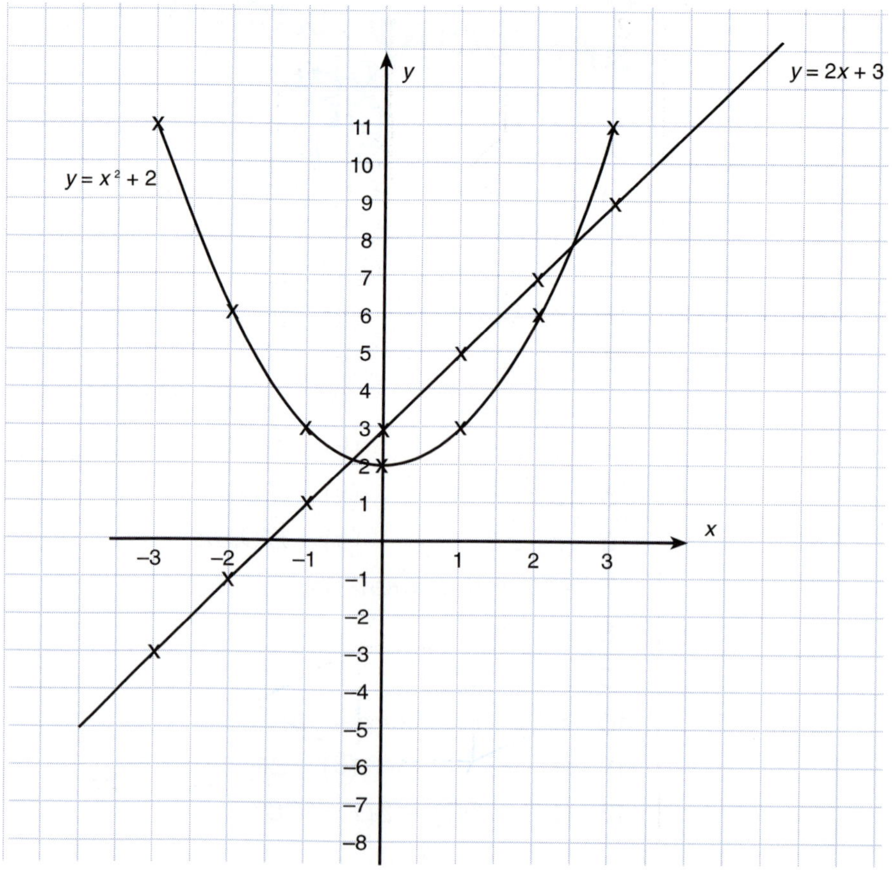

(a) $y = 2x + 3$

x	−3	−2	−1	0	1	2	3
y	−3	−1	1	3	5	7	9

(b) $y = x^2 + 2$

x	−3	−2	−1	0	1	2	3
y	11	6	3	2	3	6	11

Equations and formulae

1 (a) £229 (b) £475 (c) $C = 175 + 6p$

2 Cost = $35m$

3 32.4

4 (a) $7a$ (b) $7c$ (c) $6a + 2b$
(d) $8b$ (e) $21ab$ (f) $10a^3$

5 (a) $2x + 8$ (b) $10y - 15$ (c) $a^2 + ab$ (d) $2a^2 - 2ac$

6 (a) $n = 2$ (b) $p = 19$ (c) $a = 10$ (d) $n = 30$
(e) $x = 2$ (f) $n = 3$ (g) $y = 2$ (h) $y = 3$ (i) $x = 1$

7 $x = 10$ cm

Shape, space and measures

Properties of shape

1 Reflective, rotational and plane symmetry

2

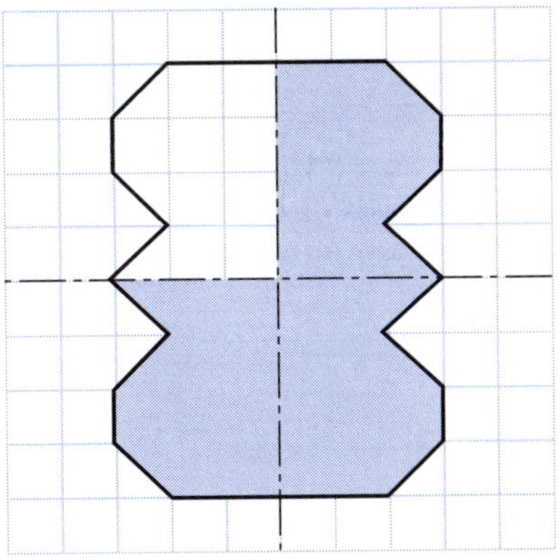

3 Check your answer with pages 50–51.

4 Octagon

5

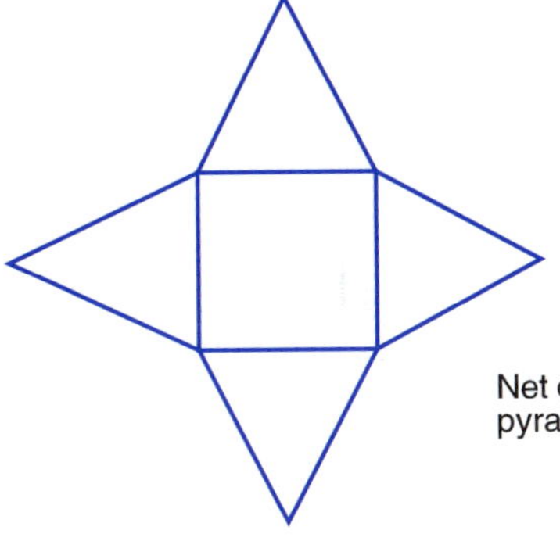

Net of a square-based pyramid

6

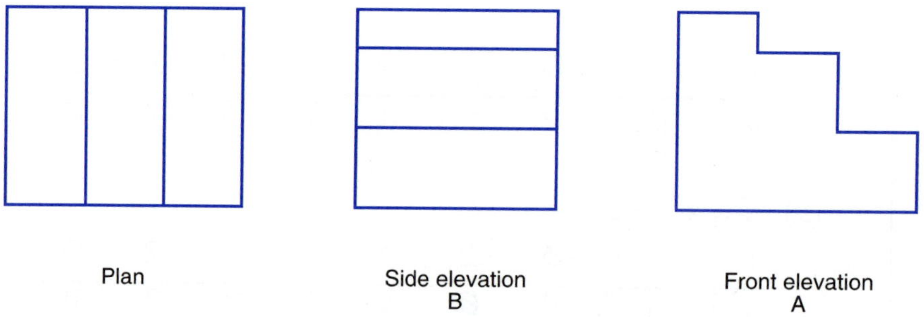

7 (a) $a = 70°$ (b) $p = 80°$
(c) $x = 40°$, $y = 140°$, $z = 140°$ (d) $a = 55°$, $b = 70°$
(e) $x = 70°$ (f) $a = 110°$, $b = 70°$, $c = 70°$
(g) $a = 50°$, $b = 50°$, $c = 130°$

Properties of position, movement and transformation

1

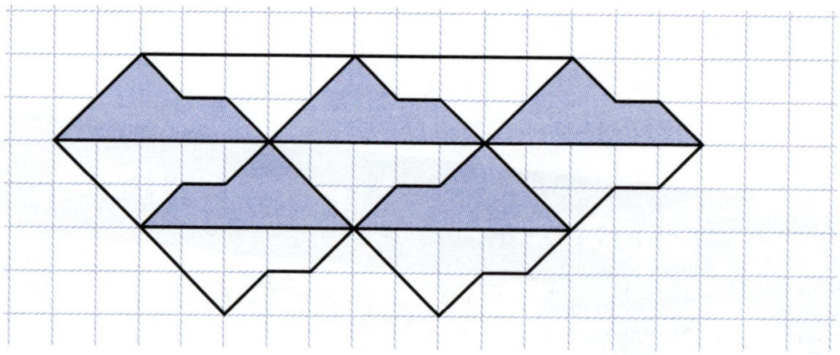

2 (a) 110° (b) 310°

3

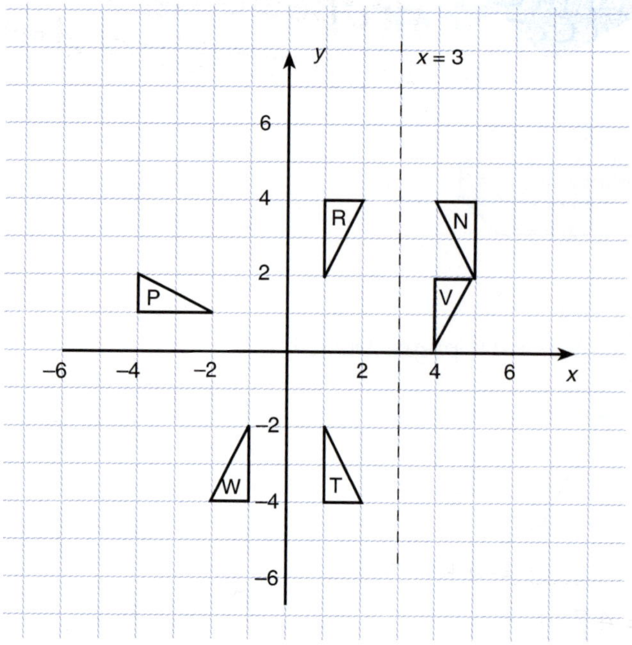

4 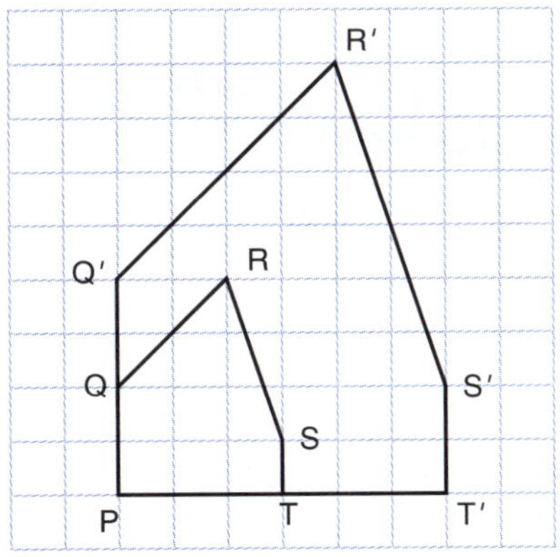

5 7 km

Measures

1 4.4 pounds

2 3.5 kg

3 5 000 ml

4 10 miles

5 12.5 cm

6 (a) A = 12.2; B = 12.8

(b) A = 14.8; B = 15.2; C = 15.6

(c) A = 20.75; B = 21.5; C = 22.25

7 (a) 48 cm^2 (b) 16 cm^2 (c) 12.4 cm^2

8 (a) 36 cm (b) 42 cm^2

9 (a) 58.8 cm^3 (b) 216 cm^3

Handling data

Processing and interpreting data

1 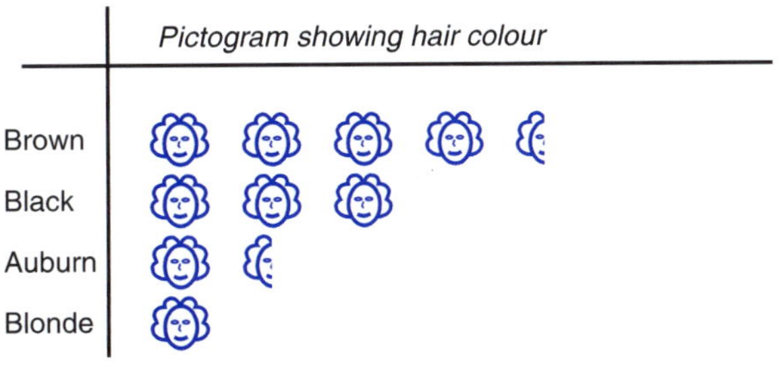

2 (a) 280 girls (b) 140 girls

3 Negative correlation

4 There are no scales and bar B is wider than bar A

5 (a) mean = 4.7 (b) median = 3

(c) mode = 2 (d) range = 12

6 Your opinion that *Neighbours* is better than *Home and Away* is evident.

Estimating and calculating the probabilities of events

1, 2 *See notes on pages 86–87.*

3 (a) $\frac{3}{7}$ (b) $\frac{4}{7}$ (c) 0

4 (a) $\frac{4}{8} = \frac{1}{2}$ (b) $\frac{5}{8}$ (c) $\frac{2}{8} = \frac{1}{4}$

5 $\frac{2}{9}$

6 96

7 $\frac{58}{320} = \frac{29}{160}$

8 (a)

Die 1	6	7	8	9	10	11	12
	5	6	7	8	9	10	11
	4	5	6	7	8	9	10
	3	4	5	6	7	8	9
	2	3	4	5	6	7	8
	1	2	3	4	5	6	7
		1	2	3	4	5	6
				Die 2			

(b) (i) $\frac{3}{36} = \frac{1}{12}$ (ii) $\frac{18}{36} = \frac{1}{2}$